LONG GONE &
LOST:

True Fictions and Other Lies

LONG GONE & LOST:

True Fictions and Other Lies

Bobby Horecka

MADVILLE PUBLISHING

Lake Dallas, Texas

FIRST EDITION

Requests for permission to reprint material from this work should be sent to:

Permissions
Madville Publishing
P.O. Box 358
Lake Dallas, TX 75065

Author Photograph: John Squyres @ Blue Media Works
Cover Design: Jacqueline Davis

ISBN: 978-1-948692-28-1 paperback, 978-1-948692-29-8 ebook
Library of Congress Control Number: 2019950605

for Jenn, my bride—

I'll never have time enough nor words to say how
much it means that you find within yourself
the strength it takes to love me . . .

—*B*—

TABLE OF CONTENTS

But I, being poor, have only my dreams;

I have spread my dreams under your feet;

Tread softly because you tread on my dreams.

—W.B. Yeats, The Wind Among the Reeds, 1899

LUBBOCK, 1974

If the stars had aligned better, the boy could've been the son of a teacher, a scientist, or a business tycoon. He might've spent his days blowing out birthday candles, playing catch outside with dad, or singing silly songs with mom, full of elaborate gestures. The itsy-bitsy spider, perhaps. Or He's Got the Whole World. That one about that bridge that kept falling down.

He'd settle for the alphabet song. Johnny Cash. Sabbath. The Doors. The son of son of a sailor. Anything, really. Was it so much to ask?

Other kids did such things. He'd seen it, out in the world, the few times he got to go. But not at this house. Never here. It could've been a fairy tale for all he knew. Make believe. Something in a faraway, near-forgotten dream.

He often swipes a grimy paw at his overgrown hair. It is forever falling in his face—pasting to one of his cheeks, poking him in the eye, or crawling up a nostril—always itching something awful. It's a blonde like you rarely see, not so much a color as a *light*. It seems to emit its own luminance, an untamed radiance of tangled muss.

Paired with those ice blue eyes and a devilish perma-grin Kool-Aid stain, he's impossible to forget. Even if he wasn't yet three and already scrawny for his age.

Those cold eyes, that wild, flame-like hair.

They burn in your soul, alive and living, as he was, beyond the outer fringe of nightmares out at reality's bitter edge. That fiery hair, those frozen eyes, consuming . . .

⁜ ⁜ ⁜

The *fuzzies* came on bouncing, bounding *footses* into his hidey spot, his hole, his safe place, beyond the *owey* pokes that make you bleed. He found it following *bunnies*. They were always outside. Light and *dawk*. Nibble, nibble. *Hawp*, hop, to over *they-yuh*.

Thems eated da gwass. The boy snatches a tuft of winter-burned stems, holds it high. Grass, he means to say. The man with long dark hair listens intently, looking on in bemused disbelief.

"No thanks," the man says, his voice deep, mellow. "I got my own."

He laughs like a whisper, airy, holds up funnel-shaped hand-rolled, the smoke curling and vanishing. Curling. Swirling. Gone. Curling. Delicate. Swirling threads. *Kitty whiskers*, the boy tried to say once, then vanished and gone.

The man never understands him.

He comes out every day and sits on the wooden steps, smokes his smoke beside the half-opened back door. Twirls of smoke vanish in the cold air. Smells so good to the boy. Not the smoke, but behind that door.

He can't tell him that. He doesn't know how. No one taught him how. But the coffee brewing, butter melting, eggs browning, sizzling bacon: the boy's insides churn each morning, his senses keen.

Like something wild. Half-starved wolf cub. Always the same.

The man never understands.

Often, at night, the boy races off in the dark. Has to, you see. Got crazy inside. He makes the red-dirt yard in seconds flat, dodging minefields of junk, rusted, jagged-edged cans, busted crates spilling broken bottle shards, sharp as razors and hidden by night. Barefoot, of course, but much safer there than he was inside. He spies the secret path deep into the thorny brush. He knows the spot well. He has used it too many times before. They never ever wake up it seems, when darkness gives way to light. They stay up moaning, screaming, fighting is what it sounds like to the boy, and it goes on all night. Don't try and wake them, though, or walk in when there's noise. They get awful mean. They just don't like little boys. Or perhaps they do—too much—that's what sets them off. But it's times like these, when they catch him, he thinks he won't make it out. They hit with belts and boards and fists, often swinging blind in the dark. Twice they'd connected when they lashed out like that, and twice they'd knocked him out.

The *Preacher*, everybody calls him, and with him always that skinny white, white pink-eyed man that everybody calls the *Ghost*. They are always trying to hurt. Just last month, the little boy stuck his finger in a door hinge, a stupid thing to do. Split his finger and his nail, got blood all everywhere. Over the next few weeks, though, it was healing. Until *Preacher* stomped it flat at church. *Ghost* grabbed his head and shoved him to the floor. That wasn't bad, though. Not until *Preacher* took his heel and ground round, mashing it hard into the floor, like he'd seen the *Hunter* do with cigarettes when he was through. He never hears anybody call *Hunter* anything. He scares everybody because he is always mean. He carries a big, bone-handled knife and had taken it to the boy once or twice. It doesn't hurt so bad, getting cut by his knife. Nothing like when they hit him instead. The last time he got hold of him, he turned his whole bed red. But the *Candyman* was hardest of all to read. One minute he'll be almost nice, the next he'll beat you half to death. And he does things, awful things, that hurt so bad. Just know you need to run hard and fast, no matter how hungry you may be, if you ever hear him ask *Want some candy, baby boy?*

So, mornings the boy always spends outside. Most days, he is already there anyway. And one day, he tried to catch a bunny. The boy thought he'd finally have a friend. They're always hopping around, nibbling on this, then hopping over there. But whenever he gets close, they run away. Run away fast. He followed it one day, down its hidden bunny trail, to see where it went. What might be there. Perhaps he'd find bunny houses, or big piles of carrots someplace. He sure could eat a few. Fuzzy warm mommy bunnies. He could go live with them. She might even sing to him. Teach him the words to that bridge song.

The spines on the bushes left him several *owies*. They burned for days and bled and bled. Took several tries to get it right, but he could run full speed and dive like Superman, his belly in the dirt. The bunny may have disappeared, no bunny house ever found, but the boy had a new hidey hole.

One even *THEY* wouldn't brave. Not *Preacher* or his *Ghost*. Not *Hunter* nor *Candyman*, even *Maybelle* and *Iris*, too. None of them get to him here, and all of them have tried. *Hunter* even tried to burn it down, with fire and a can of gas. Almost burned down that awful house instead. The boy would have been glad.

Its entrance hidden beneath sprawling boughs, pointy thorns like needles, some long as the boy's hand. Unlike before, too, when he ran out in the night, this time he brings a blanket. Probably not a blanket, really. Probably more like a towel. He isn't exactly toasty warm now, his breath hanging in white wisps about his face, but it is better than nothing. He nearly froze to death that last time without it, when the snows almost buried his boney hide, inside his secret hidey hole. Still, better than inside. He didn't dare go there. That's the fringe of nightmares . . .

Run away, if you can. It only hurts in there.

If only he had something to eat. But each time's the same. The man with long dark hair never understands.

4

✠ ✠ ✠

The man with the long dark hair considers the boy with matted fiery hair. He only appears after he's had his pain pills, dabbed the salve on the wound by his heart that never wants to heal, and lights up on the back stoop. The boy never appears until the pills kick in, until he's smoked half his smoke. Not every time, but often enough. He's not quite sure if he's even real.

Maybe it's the mix of those pills and the smoke. It doesn't help that he's always alone whenever the boy appears. His old lady said it's just a hallucination, a vision, something she read about in a book.

He just doesn't know.

The last time the boy appeared, the man with the long dark hair stuck his hand in the wound by his heart that never wants to heal. The pain was real enough. Even the boy's strange babble seemed real, too. He couldn't make it out, quite yet, but he knew he was close. His old lady, though, cooking breakfast just beyond the door, said she heard nothing, just the man with the long dark hair talking to himself.

So, that's his routine now, every day. Pills. Salve. Grass. The boy doesn't appear every day, but enough. He tries to interpret what it means when the boy appears, if it's omen or luck. He hasn't figured that out either. His old lady says it's just him, starting out the day too fucked up. He'd love to latch on to the boy, bring him inside, dangle him by one of his scrawny arms, show him to the woman beyond the door cooking breakfast. But he can't. His pain is always worse at first light. Plus, for all he knows, his hand might pass straight through. The boy, that is. But at least he'd know if he's real . . .

It doesn't help that the boy always looks the same whenever he appears, barefoot and barebacked, heavy diaper he's always hiking up. Covered in grime, always the filth, babbling away beneath his matted fiery hair. It doesn't matter, July hot or fresh fallen snow. When he appears—if he appears—it's always barebacked and barefoot.

So, he keeps his routine. Pills. Salve. Grass. Then he sits, he sits and he waits. Every day. Sometimes the boy appears; others he does not. But it's happened enough, he wonders if today will be the day.

He finds his grass in jungles far away, where he got that oozing wound by his heart that never wants to heal. It won't let him work, forever oozing. The medic told him they couldn't get it all out. "Liable to fester a while," he'd said, right before they shipped him home.

Medically discharged, but not because of that wound by his heart. No, according to the papers he had, his brain had gone bad out there in the jungles. There was a mix-up of some sort, that day in the jungle, something they called *friendly fire*. It wasn't the Slopes that shot him and left him for dead. His own sergeant, the crazy bastard, shot him.

The part that truly peeled back the man with the long dark hair was the fact he couldn't get his military award, his Purple Heart. Wounded in battle, he was, right there by his heart. They discharged him at the capitol, when all was said and done, him and his bad brain. The first stop he made, down back alley street, was a seedy old pawnshop. He got him his heart, purple and proud, an ornament made for another man's wound. But still he wore it on whatever he had on that day. Some days, there on his stoop as he plays out his routine, he'll have only a blanket draped on his shoulders, like a cape. And always—every time—if you look close and hard, you'll see that gold medallion, it's ribbon purple and white, pinned to the blanket he bled on that night.

He'd left DC for California in a second-hand car, his pills, his salve, his purple heart, and his smoke. When his wheels gave out, just half the way there, he hit the local paymaster, withdrew his combat pay, and decided to stay there. He bought him the little wood-frame house, with the stoop where he now sits, right on the edge of town. Right on the fringe of madness and nightmare, it turns out. His yard is haunted by a small, babbling boy. Or maybe, just maybe, the jungle has indeed clouded his mind.

He wishs he knew of some way he could really tell.

Looka! The boy, commanding the attention of the man with long dark hair, hops, circular in the snow. Barefooted, bare-backed. Filthy. Just the heavy diaper he has to hike up. He stops hopping. He points, stamping a tiny foot.

Looka, fuzzies house.

The man with the long dark hair and the wound by his heart, shrugs his shoulders.

"I don't understand, little man," he says. "What is it you're trying to say?"

The little boy looks up at the man, whose long dark hair is tied in back to make a tail. Most of it lies on his right shoulder, but falls behind him, strand by strand, each time he shrugs and takes another long drag. He never understands. As the boy kicks his bare foot, he hears another whispery laugh from the top of the stairs, the man with the long dark hair, sitting on his stoop, beside an open back door.

It visibly bothers the boy, that much is clear to the man. It frustrates him, this talking gap. The boy stares at the ground, hikes that heavy diaper again, left-handed, while a grimy right bats the tangled sticky bangs from his eyes. Arm twists, pretzels. He rocks the knuckles of that grimy right, back, forth, back, forth. Thinking.

He wants words. So much to say. Doesn't know how.

The boy stops sudden. Frozen, head cocked. Listening. His hands out, fingers spread. Elbows at forty-fives. Angled and frozen. The man with the long dark hair listens. He hears something, too, maybe four or five houses down. The places get progressively worse, the farther down the road. His wood frame house, although not very large, is a palace in comparison to some of those at the end of the road. If it's coming from one of those places, no wonder the little ghost boy seems so scared.

An old screen door opens, the popping thrumming sound of the door spring stretching, the needs-oil creak of a rusted hinge. The sound of someone stepping out, followed by the familiar pop, wood smacking wood when the spring snaps back. A crisp new sound rings out on the cold morning air, the *chingle* of shattering glass. The man with the long dark hair looks down at the little boy. He, still frozen, a tiny statue, unmoving. Well, not entirely unmoving, he appears to be keeping tabs of each new crash of glass.

"Aw man," the man with the long dark hair says. "I didn't know we were—"

The boy silences the man with the long dark hair, popping up his hand like a traffic cop. The boy cocks his head, listening. From the sound of it, someone is getting rid of a whole box of bottles. But these aren't typical beer bottles. They sound larger, heavier, like wine bottles, or pop bottles. Surely, they won't dispose of them. Those are worth money, probably a buck or two by now, the man estimates.

The ringing stops. A deep smoker's hack rings out.

"Oh-oh," the little boy with matted fiery hair says, not at all loud, but clear and distinct. His sergeant, the one who shot him, had a voice like that.

"I galla go," the boy says, but before he vanishes from sight, the man with long dark hair suddenly perks up, snaps fingers, and points at the boy. "You said you gotta go!"

The boy smiles, mimics his point. Some other time, maybe, he'll teach him that snap. He looks back to where all the noise had come from, four or five houses down, cautious at first, peeking inch by inch around the corner.

Then wink-quick, seeing it clear, he bolts round the trees and is gone.

The man with the long dark hair sucks at the nubbin, but just as he is about to flick his roach down to the red dirt, a very thin, very pale, very unusual man walks up, slow and quiet, craning his neck this way and that, checking the space between the houses. Something about him, the way he moves—the man with long dark hair can't put his finger on it—is just off. Unusual.

The man with long dark hair hardly breathes. The only thing moving, aside from the thin silver line of smoke rising, curling into the sky, is the wounded soldier's eyes. The pale man, rail thin, has a thick navy coat, the kind you see on men working the docks. Red corduroy pants, poking out from below the coat, twig thin.

Seeing him, dressed so warmly, only lent credence to the impossibility of the boy. Plus, this fellow pulls the top of his coat tighter, as if, despite all those clothes, he is still cold. There's no way that a baby in diapers and nothing else could possibly be out here. Barefoot and barebacked. Besides, pale as this cat is, he's probably just another backyard premonition. It's why he looks so damn weird. His face, pale as snowfall, could've been whittled from wood for all the expression it held. He'd be impossible to beat at Five Card Stud, face like that.

And very thin. Very pale. Very unusual.

The fellow keeps scanning the ground, this way then that, like a pigeon following an old man round a park, looking for handouts from that bag of popcorn he smells. Would've thought he passed by earlier and dropped his favorite dollar. The man with long dark hair stays statue-still, moving nothing but his eyes, which stay glued on the pale man, who falls flat to the ground, as if his drill sergeant just hollered to give him twenty. He never gets around to the push or the up. Rather, he stays down there a good minute and a half, at least, staring deep in the darkness underneath the house.

Just as the man with the long dark hair decides to ask the dude if he's OK, he rocks on his knee and stands back up, moves on to his house to peer at its underside. Before he does, though, the unusually pale man notices a blue metal five-gallon can there at the foot of the stairs. The man with the long dark hair watches the pale man open it up, remove a combat boot that's inside. The pale man squints his eyes, peering at the boot.

The man with the long dark hair has had enough: "Morning," he says. The pale man jumps. He had no clue the man was there, but it has positively no impact on the color of his cheeks. They're practically clear.

He mumbles something.

"What was that?" asks the man with long dark hair.

Through a significant hair-lip, the pale man speaks: "Have you seen a little boy come by here?"

He's seen him, too. But how? The man with the long dark hair doesn't understand. He rises and steps through the half-open door, closes it behind him, and bolts the lock.

The little boy with fiery matted hair disappears in the brush long before *Ghost* wanders over. He decides to go exploring, down Bunny Biways, trails running this way and that, all over the ground, like a tangled-up net. Intertwining, Bunny internet.

Then there comes a loud sound, like a bucket of gravel dumping on an old tin roof. The boy goes toward it, having never heard anything like it before. Not knowing what the sound is, he comes up slowly, keeps his cover in the in brush. He lets out a small squeal from his spot in the trees when he sees. *The Fuzzies!* All there in a pile, all playing and biting and—wait a minute—what are they biting?

The boy stands at the edge of the brush, checking for people. He's not sure who here he can trust. He looks as far as he can one way, then spins round the other way, checking, ever so careful. He doesn't want to be found.

It appears the coast is clear.

He doesn't relate the two, what he sees with the noise that he's heard, but his buddies, the *fuzzies*, are all there.

Someone laid the lid to a trashcan in the middle of the red dirt yard and in its center, piled nice and high, is what looks like a cereal of some sort, the kind that comes with a toy. The *fuzzies* sure seem to like them. And the boy's so hungry . . .

"Gots any fo' me?" the boy asks the fuzzy little dogs, all too immersed in their meal to pay much mind to the boy. He walks behind them to the huge serving tray and sits right down in the middle of all his fuzzy friends where he can reach the pile, too. His buddies all round him don't mind in the least. And the boy can't be happier. He is surrounded by his little buddies and they have something to eat. The cereal they eat could sure use some milk because it is awful dry. It doesn't have much of a taste either. But this is his first food in a couple of days. Now he can tell the man with long dark hair how his buddies, the *fuzzies*, had found him a feast.

So there, surrounded by eight little mongrel pups, the baby boy and baby dogs form quite a sight, especially when he points his diapered butt up to the sky so he can eat like his friends. For once in his life he looks like the biggest pup in the pack.

And as he swallows kibble, there in the yard, wouldn't you know it? He let down his guard.

The boy in the house is looking out the window while his momma warms up some chicken soup for him and his brother from a can. Why the woman bothers with such non-sense like heating it he'll never understand. She stands there stirring, stirring, stirring for like ten minutes. Then it sits on the table for next to forever, so it can cool off enough to eat. What a waste! So, while she stirs, stirs, stirs over the stove, the boy watches as another boy wanders into his yard, plops next to his dogs, and eats their food.

"Momma, there's a baby outside eating with the dogs."

"Sure there is, honey. What's his name?
"I don't know. I was gonna ask you."
"That's nice honey . . . Listen, mamma needs to make a phone call. Why don't you go get your brother so y'all can get going."

She grabs the receiver and dials her number, dial whirling, again and again. They wash up like they've been told. The elder of the two finishes faster, wipes his hands on his pants. When the smaller one comes, he joins his brother, looking out the window.

"Whatcha looking at?"
"A baby."
"Nu-*uh*."
"Uh-*huh*. He was eating their food walla-go," big brother says.
"*Nuh uh!*"
"*Uh huh!*"
"*Mom!*"

If only the stars were better aligned. . . .

HAP
HAZ
ARD

I remember a boy
clumsy, cotton-topped

following that old man
around, every-where

hat stuffed with newspapers
hulking, over-sized

trying desperate to fit in
uncertain, hap-hazard

bottle feeding orphan calves
tugging, love-starved

nourishing pink nipples
rubber, man-made

served up by little lad's hand
clumsy, cotton-topped

for all know motherless, eventually
orphans, other-wise

Hiccups

Beyond the open window, it's early evening, Saturday. The sun hangs lazy to the west, as the first hints at reprieve from the stifling summer heat creep from long shadows. Mowers, now silent, drip dry in outbuildings, the whole neighborhood fresh mowed, while cicadas unwind electric buzz from hidden boughs in the lush tree canopy, playing along to the percussive pulse of metallic Rain King sprinklers. Inside, the tiny light-haired boy giggles, splashes and slaps at the bubbly froth of his bath. Some might call him towheaded. Cottontopped. Truth is, light is most apt, truest to its airy, luminous aura, even all wet and plastered to his scalp.

A woman walks in, arms full of technicolored towels. She sees him and stops a while to watch. He fascinates her, always absorbed in his imaginings, conjuring entire villages of characters, personalities and situations from absolute nothing. Perhaps not nothing entirely, but close. She's noticed already he needs barely a glimpse of something to fold it into his playtime depictions, an ever-evolving world of storylines he acts out with his toys. Where he comes up with half of it, she never knows.

The boy, still a newcomer to her home, is swift approaching his first six months there, barely any time at all by her way of thinking. For the boy, however, this current stretch marks the longest he's lived anyplace in his rather brief life. He spent his first few days with her downright bewildered people ever come back to someplace they'd left behind after going to church, for instance, or even the grocery store. Not long after he arrived there, she found him trying to load all his toys in her car so he wouldn't have to leave them behind.

The woman leans back in the door frame, towels resting on her slender hip, simply listening and watching the boy. *Her* boy. Chores can wait.

She's slight, pretty, and not yet thirty. Between her elvish, light brown hair, always kept short, her faded bellbottom jeans and that flowy, leaf-print blouse hanging halfway down her thighs, she could pass for a Partridge Family stand-in if you handed her a guitar or tambourine. Perhaps even Shirley Jones herself, if you talked her out of those wide, round-framed eyeglasses she always wears But it's the little light-haired boy who holds her fascination. Moments like these, she's certain, she'll never forget all her life.

After several minutes of watching him splash about, she glances at her watch. *The Muppets*, his favorite show, will begin soon. It's time to wrap up.

"Make sure you get clean," she says.

The little boy jumps, startled she's there, then beams when he sees her, sounds his giggly laugh. "Mommy, you *sca*-yud, me!"

The woman can't help but smile. They can work on *R*-sounds another day. Right now, it sounds ridiculously cute coming from the little guy.

"You better hurry or you're going miss Kermit and Fozzie the Bear."

He dives with abandon, filling both hands with suds. He slaps them to his face and rubs, maniacal. "All done!" he says.

"Let's seeeee," the woman says. She sets the towels on the countertop and steps toward the tub. "Did you scrub yoouurr . . . (The boy hunches down, playful eyes shimmering. He's ready to bolt, any second, any direction) . . . *KNEE?*"

"Uh-*HUH!*" he lies. Aside from his face, seconds ago, nothing on him has been scrubbed since she did it, last week, when he coated himself in mud. She knows this, but honesty lessons can wait, too. It's just a game. *Their* game, no less.

"Did you scrub yoouurr . . . (She strikes a thinking pose, finger to chin) . . . *BUTT?*"

He giggles at the word. "Uh-*HUH*," he lies again.

"How about your . . . (She's close enough to tickle whatever she names and this is the boy's favorite part; he hunches tighter, a constant giggle going in anticipation) . . . *NECK?*"

He hunches shoulders, scrunches tiny neck, giggling. "Uh-*HUH!*"

"How about youurrrr . . . (Her hand drops beneath bubbles quick enough to snag a bass swimming) . . . *TOES?*"

He kicks wildly, giggles more. "Uh-*HUH!*"

"How about your . . . (Tickling) . . . *POOPECK?*"

Another funny word. He squeals, sheer delight, both hands at his bellybutton, Pillsbury's half-starved nephew. "Uh-*HUH!*"

"Alright, Kermit-the-Frog time! Don't forget the stopper."

The little light-haired boy laps his bath in victory, arms raised. First clockwise, then counter, mouth open wide, rasping out stadium noise. The woman grabs a towel, bright red, shakes it open. It's barely spread before the boy dives, the rattle of the stopper's dog tag chain on porcelain resonates and echoes. He tips the woman backward onto her bottom. She crosses her legs, Indian-style, rubs his head good, then drapes him in red fluff. She hugs him, tight. He nestles close, craving her warmth. They linger, woman and child, perfect and precious.

"Mommy?" his tiny voice muffled in towel.

"Yes?"

Silence. He's rock still. She digs at the towel, finds his face. His eyes, red from bathtub shenanigans, are glazed and unfocused, brooding and dark—a thousand miles away—nearly trancelike. Makes her skin crawl.

"What is it?"

His focus returns at the sound of her voice, his eyes peer up at her face.

"Can I ask you a question?"

His voice, uncertain. He curls even tinier.

"You just did," she says, smiling.

The boy turns away, eyes on the floor tiles beyond her lap. He squirms, face twisted. Impatient? Perplexed? She can't tell.

"What is it? You can tell me."

He squirms again. Fingers piddling on the opposing palm, his eyes shift, searching. Words elude him. He tries: "Well . . ."

She waits.

He squirms more, eyes back on the cold tile.

"Really, it's OK. Tell me."

He fidgets more, avoiding her eyes. Squirming, finally, to the edge of her lap, her knee the perfect height from the floor. His little legs bent at right angles; feet soundly shored. His full back now to her, he slumps tiny shoulders as he blurts it out, eyes pinched shut.

"When's Daddy gonna put his pee-pee in my mouth?"

He slumps even lower, the words out there, now gone.

The woman tenses, full body. The boy feels it.

It scares him. His head swivels, eyes wide, over shoulder. His eyes glisten, uncertain, on the brink of tears. He doesn't recognize the strange look she wears—her jaw, set; cheeks, drawn; lips, pursed. It scares him. Even her eyes are different, more open, the white parts more visible. Her focus is now on the floor tiles, down and away, searching. Their typical twinkle, lost. It scares him even more.

His little lip quivers, as tears streak his cheeks. He twists full round, dives face-first at her lap. Tiny arms snuggle around the woman's beltline. Breath choppy, body shuddering, he sobs, then bleats, towel-muffled: "I'm *SAW*eeeee!"

Her neck jerks, stunned. Such extremes, such questions, and he's just three.

She knows, too that she's to blame for his bawling. She has no poker face. Her heart controls all her expression. Still, it's so random. So gut-tumbling. So unexpected.

He's only *three*, after all.

The woman strokes his back, tender and consoling, then closes her eyes, and sits—steady stroking—on the floor, Indian-style. She breathes deep, filling lungs until she can't—ever stroking—then releases breath through parted lips, slow and deliberate. Lungs emptied, she opens her eyes, face transfigured, much softer than moments ago.

Done stroking, she runs fingers through his downy hair. It's almost dry already. He's calm again, quiet. His face still buried in her lap. The harsh bathroom light gleams on his bare bottom. She's compelled to cover him, tugging at the towel now balled beneath him.

She breathes deep once more, chooses careful words.

"You never have to worry about anything like that here."

Her voice holds, soft and steady, as she asks, "Why did you ask me that?"

Her faces twists, not wanting to know. Not *really*. The boy, still face-down in her lap and buried in towel, sucks snot, then begins: "Caw bawmben dawlash mooawgoodie . . ."

Words, completely indecipherable, but he never stops. She pulls red folds from his face.

". . . he peed on my *ee*-yahs (snuff) and then he made me stand in the snow it was *ev*-wee-*wa*yah, and then . . ."

She couldn't make him talk earlier. She can't make him stop now. He slaughters every *R* and tops each horrifying new detail with another "*and then*," which makes that last bit sound like a church social. The more the boy talks, too, the more the woman realizes that it isn't some isolated incident, but an ongoing, serial molestation of a baby boy by what sounds like a dozen or so *people*, men and women both.

How unlucky can one kid get? First, his own mom dies, in her twenties, and in a hospital of all places. His grandma, soon after. The woman's husband was the brother of the little boy's birth mother.

It only makes sense that they give him someplace to stay. He should be with blood kin.

Still, food's one thing, so's a roof overhead. This is entirely something else . . .

Doubt fills her. How could she ever handle it?

She looks at the boy, still talking, still all-new "*and thens.*"

He did it, she thinks. Somehow, he handled it. And he's only three.

Something he says catches her ear. One of those things sounded recent, extremely so, as in just a few months. Since the state intervened. Placed him in their so-called *care.* Her stomach knots. Disgusted disbelief.

They criticized her every move. Her husband's. For weeks on end, always taking him away, delivering him to perfect strangers. Strangers who would do such things to a boy . . .

My God, is *that* what he just said?

At a *church social?* What kind of people—

All from the mouths of a babes, no less. Her baby boy. It is too much.

". . . and they had a *wheel* mean dog (snuff) he *bited* me . . . see?"

The boy twists—contorts, jelly-boned—to show her his elbow, under now atop, outer turning in, like rubber. He inspects every inch of elbow, eyes crossing, close enough to lick, if he wanted. But nothing. Not even a scar. Puzzled, he checks his other arm, just in case, twisting and contorting. Not there either.

"*Way*-uh did it go?"

The woman, preoccupied in her own thoughts, doesn't answer.

His interest wanes. Tears long since dried like his hair, it's time to move on. He sniffles, saws an arm beneath his nose.

"Mommy, you gonna watch *Kuhmie* da *Fwog* with me? Will ya, Mommy?"

He buries a finger up his nostril, clean to the root. He blinks hopeful eyes, awaiting answers. The boy, finally quiet, still, the woman snaps back.

Towel in a wad by the wall, fallen during elbow inspection, she has a hard time seeing beyond his nakedness. Eden's forbidden fruit of knowledge that she'll never unlearn.

"You need to get dressed," she says.

"OK." He hops up, flutters his tongue and bolts out of the bathroom. Then, halfway down the hallway, she hears the rest. "Beep! Beep!"

She sits in the bathroom, the middle of the floor, unable to move.

Just can't.

How does he do it? Switch gears. Switch it off like a light. The woman never would.

These moments, she was certain, she'd never forget. Not ever. Not for the rest of her life.

In that respect, she envies the boy.

"Mommy . . . Mom-*MAH!*" his voice piercing, echoing, but definitely down the hall.

"What is it, sweetie?"

"Can I *WAY*-yah my mo-*tah*-cycle jammies?"

"Sure."

"OK . . ."

"*Patatatathhh!* Beep, beep!"

The woman finally gets off the floor, long after the *Muppets* played their music and finished their show, apparently. The boy, *her* boy, is fast asleep in her bed.

But she is still reeling.

She glares at the mirror. *What did you get yourself into?* She mouths the words, silent, at her reflection. Hardly words the boy ever need hear. It racks her in guilt. But how would she ever get beyond this? How could she tell her family? Or even her husband?

She'll need to rob a bank for his therapy bills. Last thing they need right then.

Guilt sets in again. Then, it's gone, replaced with a pure white, seething rage.

Critical of *HER* every move yet sidestepping each question she asked about the boy's past. "It's privileged," they'd say, over and over. Nothing more. Not until they were leaving, the boy standing right there, did they ever offer anything more.

"He may have a few . . . *hiccups* . . . he'll need to work through."

That's exactly how she said it, too; those big pauses all around such a peculiar word. It vexed her. Such an unusual, unimportant, insignificant word. Compared to what the boy just shared with her, it was. You'd think baby boys standing around in the goddam snow like some sort of demented sundae would at least rate something a little more serious, more legitimate, than *hiccups*. Wouldn't you think?

Maybe they didn't know. It would be so much easier to bear. But why, then, had they chosen such a peculiar turn of phrase?

"He may have a few . . . *hiccups* . . . he'll need to work through."

Don't kid yourself, you *know* they *KNEW!* They knew damn good and well. And they did nothing to help him. Nothing at all. *Hiccups!* They're probably dumping off some other poor kid with that same pervert molester right now. Or feeding some other unsuspecting parent some bizarre, meaningless phrase.

HICCUPS!

She could've snatched that woman's head bald.

She stares at the angry woman reflected, then reaches

for the light switch, and it hits her. Her entire body lurches, throat burning, while a tiny *UP!* escapes her lips.

"For real? You have got be (*UP!*) kidding me."

She turns on a faucet. As she glares in the mirror once again, the words to a rhyme suddenly pop into her mind. Her mother taught her the words in their native Czech, when she was no bigger than the boy is now.

Třikrát je zavolali do	(Three times they called)
(*UP!*) Třpytivého skla	(into a glittering glass)
Černý ďábel na ně	(Black Devil on them)
Déšť kletby z nebe (*UP!*)	(Rain curses from heaven)

It frightened her, then, as it does now, still. Hairs crawl on her neck. She hadn't thought of it in years (*UP!*) probably wouldn't have now, were it not so damn appropriate. She sips water, crawls into bed beside her boy. Her hiccups pass, eventually, as they usually do. She prays only the boy's someday will, too. And she sleeps fitful, left-on lights keeping her from dreams . . . .

CHICKEN HAWK DOWN

"Drive!" the old man yelled, sliding across the hood, Duke Boy-style, to skirt past meandering cows, then pulling his weather-beaten twenty-two from its window rack behind the torn bench seat and leaping into the truck bed over the beefy, mud-flecked rear fenders of his olive green 1965 Chevrolet. With a couple easy steps and a casually placed elbow on the cab's roof, he looked like he had just strolled into a beer joint, his favorite song on the jukebox, and bought the whole place a round. Pulled it off so smooth, too. You'd sworn he did stuff like that every day.

Pity my saucered eyes and slacked jaw got wasted just then. Together, they had to've made for one of my best *Holy Crap!* faces, ever. Who could've guessed that whole slide gag was just Grampa's warm-up act?

Mom, meanwhile, ground through gears like she had a spare set in her purse, that old truck not budging an inch despite all the racket. Grampa suddenly hunkered down like he was bracing for a wave. "Hang on!" he shouted, palming his backwards khaki cap tight to his scalp, and poking his tongue out the side of his lip as he worked that old rifle like a giant gear-shifter, matching Mom's each new gear grind note for note.

I couldn't help it. I giggled right out loud. I did that a lot with Grampa.

He shot me one of his great stiff-lipped smirks as he straightened back up. No sooner than he did, though, he cringed at one of Mom's extra loud grinds, shoulders and face

23

all scrunched up, knee lifting. That set me off on another gig-gling fit, one cut short when the truck lurched forward about half a foot, backfired and died. Good thing I'd grabbed the side rail when Grampa told me to or I'd 've tumbled right out the back. Mom instantly cranked the engine, gas fumes suddenly thick in my nose. Grampa waved me up beside him and then cocked his head sideways to peer through the back glass at Mom. Sounded like she was trying to strangle the poor thing back to life, while all sorts of angry words spewed forth—none I could make out from where I was, mind you; not there, in the back—but I bet I'd've gotten an education riding shotgun, up there with her.

All I heard, from where I was, was the angry. Kinda glad I wasn't up there, to be honest. But I wasn't about to test fate twice, either, nor was I gonna wait around for Grampa to change his mind on that whole stand-by-me request. In no time flat, I was right beside his pantleg. That whole lurch combined with the cannon blast a few moments ago still had my heart racing. I couldn't have been more than seven and maybe fifty pounds—if you rolled me in flour and gave me a couple of big rocks to hold—and half the size he was.

Grampa hollered something at Mom that sounded like *Pudge Ebway, the moth's down,*[1] which meant positively *noth-ing* to me. It'd be years still before I could make out a lick of that Czech they were always prattling at one another. And Mom was no help. She stayed stone silent, blood rising in her cheeks. Grampa smiled down at me then, his blue eyes twinkling like stars on a clear country night.

He and Mom had the best eyes, especially when they were up to no good, which for Grampa, was most of the time. We never got around to it that day, but sometimes when we finished those late evening feedings, Grampa and

---

1 What Grampa probably said was *Potřebujete pomoc tam,* which is Czech for *Need some help up there?* Either way, this version or *Pudge Ebway,* Mom still held her tongue.

me, we'd lay back on his old truck as he pointed out constellations and told me stories. I'd probably looked up at those twinkling lights a lot more than most kids my age, but they transformed amazingly with him as my guide.

Most days, too, Grampa looked half-crippled, walking across our farm. He had a catch in his back and a limp that fit him better than the baggy workpants he wore. He was probably pushing sixty then, but age had nothing to do with how he walked. He was healthy as they came. A constant outdoorsman since he was my size, he thought nothing of fording a creek, tossing gas on a fire or shimmying up a tree. That probably had a lot to do with how he hurt himself. Explained the catch in his back, anyway.

It definitely came from climbing a tree, though. Well, maybe not *climbing*, precisely. *Falling* would be a better word. And boy, did he ever. But before I tell you about Grampa's fall, you probably ought to know him a little better first. *He'd* insist on it, anyway.

His father built a sprawling house on the farm Grampa would later call his own. He raised a dozen children in that house, Grampa included. It was also where his dad conducted all his business dealings. Livestock. Grain. Cotton. That's about all most folks would have seen as legitimate businesses back then. Unless you ran a store or diner, a garage or boarding establishment, or built things for your living, everything else was considered fluff back then. Although Grampa's dad might've been just another immigrant farmer like the rest, he was also an educated man. He read and wrote music—entire symphonies, in fact, with notes drawn up to include every horn—and he stayed well-read, subscribing to all the papers from all the towns near where they lived. He also owned one of the most impressive libraries around. A consummate letter writer with extravagant penmanship, he wrote regularly to folks back home, which kept him informed on the goings-on in the Old World, as well. I found several bundles of them one day, snooping around these old trunks Grampa kept in the barn rafters, all lashed together with twine. Grampa told me his father would often read them, aloud, for friends and family members who gathered regularly at their home. And because letters tend to be a bit one-sided, he often wrote out duplicates of the letters he sent them. It sounded more like a conversation that way, Grampa said, a lot more interesting for everybody gathered there. Grampa told me it wasn't uncommon for him to have twenty or thirty people over at his house for these reading parties until all hours of the night. Assisted, no doubt, by the fact his father also made his own beer, whisky and wine throughout the Prohibition—and didn't do a half bad job of it, from what I heard—but that was never brought up in any of those stories Grampa told me. Not that it matters much, I guess. The only reason I bring it up is that it helps explain some, I think, what made my grampa tick, his seeming disregard for everything that was necessarily proper. That, and his father actually wrote enough to fill a whole trunk and bothered hanging on to it like that. Because *Grampa* never would. He might've kept old coffee cans filled with bent, rusty nails, insisting I use them whenever I worked on something around the place when I got older. But letters and writings and books, Grampa would just as soon wipe his butt with it as read it. Not in a rude way, but once he got a letter or greeting card, that object had served its purpose. The only reason he held on to the pages in that trunk was out of respect to his dad. They'd been important to him. A few years down the road, once the pages got bit more brittle and the barn rats finally gnawed a few more holes through that trunk to get at the warm dry bedding inside, Grampa wouldn't even blink at the history lost in those pages when that trunk got used for kindling.

His dad also founded one of Texas' first Czech musical groups, the Worthing Brass Band, (so named for the community where they lived) and soon earned a fine living on his music alone, playing festivals and weddings clear down to the Rio Grande Valley, to hear Grampa tell it, for he, too, was a member of that band. Still, he kept farming like always, leaving the work to that army of children he had. It made him a man of some means, especially back then, so it wasn't uncommon, either, for local politicos to stop by his place, for his blessing and campaign dime. He and a neighbor even ponied up materials and donated land along their shared property lines to open, and later, expand upon, the area's first school, Vysehrad[2] which still teaches students in grades kindergarten through eight, out there in the country. Grampa's dad died several years before I was born, so all I knew about him came from stories told by someone else. Still, I have no problem saying that Grampa was nothing like his dad. Grampa could read and play music. He played bass horns most of the time—tuba, sousaphone, baritone—and was known to piddle about on trumpet, or *trubka* in Grampa's native tongue, even if he couldn't make sense of all those damn treble clef notes. Although born in Texas and forced to speak English at school, Grampa still spoke mostly Czech, though he could and did speak English just fine. He and I couldn't've communicated otherwise. From what I hear tell, though, his father never did. He wouldn't *stoop* to speaking English. It was beneath him. Didn't even want to hear those other words uttered under his roof. He was even admired for his obstinance. And well into my lifetime, folks from the communities near that farm—El Campo, Hallettsville, La Grange, Moulton, Schulenburg, Shiner, Sweet Home,

2 Wikipedia contributors, "Vysehrad" (Wikipedia, 2018). Czech for *upper castle.* Vysehrad is a historic fort located in the city of Prague, built on the right bank of the Vltava River. Historically, it defended the city from countless attacks and served as home to many Czech nobles. Considering how the school is set atop a hill overlooking the right bank of Smothers Creek, the nearest natural waterway, I don't doubt that those who saw the one in Prague at some point were the reason the school got named what it did.

and Weimar, to name a few—were still more likely to speak Czech than any English word.

Other than a love of music and a common language, however, similarities between Grampa and his dad pretty much stopped right there. Grampa left school after eighth grade, not uncommon back then, but hardly soon enough for him. He never liked reading much, and if he ever wrote more than it took to fill in a check or mark the date a calf was born on the drugstore calendar by the kitchen table, I don't recall it.

Grampa preferred a life of doing things to reading about them. He hunted. He fished. And he farmed. He worked as hard as he played, and if he had his druthers, he did it all outside. He loved the land where he was raised and never strayed far from it. It occurred to me, years later, he never went *anyplace* he couldn't get there and back from in a single day's drive. He had friends but was hardly a socialite, and he happily left all the politicking and business dealings to his brother Blase, the war hero turned businessman, who lived on the property adjoining his, next door to his store and dancehall. "Politics ain't nothing but a headache," Grampa told me once, "nothing but a bunch of *zkažený* snakes, *Černá* cheats, and *falešný* ph'losophers."[3] Then, he spat on the bare dirt as if to punctuate it. I bet if Grampa could've taken his weekly communion out there in the woods by the deer feeder, unbothered and alone, he would've. He lived his whole life right there. The cradle they placed him in as a newborn and his deathbed no more than a few feet apart, when all was said and done. He liked it there, so it suited him just fine.

Unfortunately, his father's big sprawling house didn't hold up near as well. It was no slouch, by any means. Eighty years, it stood, at least, which ain't bad for an old pier and

---

3 Using this bastardized half-Czech, half-English language he picked up in his later years to communicate with those like me who didn't know Czech, what he said was "nothing but *corrupt* snakes, *illicit* cheats and *fake philosophers*," that final word he always pronounced with just three syllables.

beam, wood-frame place. Even then, parts might've settled wonky and it needed a fresh coat of paint, but it was still a good house. I hear tell it killed two different dozers when they finally brought it down. Why they did it exactly, I don't know, but if it'd been me, I think I would've done it so I could finally get out of its shadow.

I still remember that massive wrap-around porch, with ornate accent trim up by the roof, all hand-crafted by Grampa's dad, I was told. They laced the corners at each of those hand-tooled, solid wood columns holding the roof up. I think the pattern was meant to be leaves of some sort, but I always thought they were angel wings. The entire decking was set way above my head back then, five feet up at least, with these great stairs set right at the corner, the posts of its railing tooled to look just like the pillars on the porch. Grampa told me once that you could walk right off its edge and straight onto a horse. I wouldn't know. The only horses I ever saw out there were the ones that came by—usually when it was cold and rainy out, the horses and riders both looking about half dead and miserable—on the trail ride from someplace down in the Valley to the Houston livestock show. I remember trying to climb on Major, Grampa's massive German shepherd that went with us everywhere, not long after I saw those riders the first time. I kept falling off, though, until Major spun around and nipped me good. I didn't try again after that.

Grampa told me he sold a horse once for just five dollars, back when he was a kid. I remember not believing that story at first, but it would be years before I could wrap my head around what it must've been like living through Great Depression. Toss in the fact that Gramma acted like horses were just about the filthiest beasts on the planet. Worse than flies, and she always killed every one of those she saw with this wire-handled swatter she kept within handy reach. Horses stank, she told me, "always leaving—how do you say—*sviňák*—no, *hovno*—all over."[4] Other than that, I wouldn't learn much else about horses until I was grown and on my own.[5]

The absolute best part about that porch, though, had to be the big old swing it had, hung from the rafters with these old chains. I couldn't hardly climb onto it without help, and I most certainly couldn't make it go. But, with Grampa on one side and Mom on the other, a nice steady breeze always on our faces, they'd pump a foot, one on either side, in unison, and it took off. Felt like we launched smooth off that porch, right on past the pecan tree canopy with its big pointy leaves, and just kept soaring, straight past the clouds and the moon, until the stars were so close you could reach out and palm them from the sky. Those chains sang, like the voice of God himself, rumbling and resonating you through and through, and pulled us back to the land of mortal men, slow and steady, they groaned their deep creaking voice again to send us back again. I tell you, sitting there on that porch, Grampa on one side and Mom on the other, cool breeze on my face, the gentle sway of the leaves dancing in the trees, the slow creak of those chains each time they swung back the other way. There wasn't a better spot in the whole world.

I don't know what heaven's like or if it even exists, but I sure hope it has a porch. And a swing, just like that one.

Those floors set as high as they were, steady breeze always blowing like it was, especially a big ol' place like that, it wasn't terribly surprising that someone might've thought a tie-down cable here or there might not be a bad idea. That they somehow lashed it to that massive oak at the back of the old place,

---

4   Both *sviňák* and *hovno* are Czech words for feces or shit. As I recall, both Mom and Grampa chuckled it up hearing Gramma say such a thing. Usually, foul language wasn't her thing. There she was, though, all matter-of-fact about it.

5   For the record, Gramma was right, even if I didn't understand her back then. Horses *do* indeed stink, mainly because they shit *everywhere*.

was somewhat questionable, as far as storm anchors go. And that it was a good twenty feet off the ground kinda made one wonder how they managed to get it up there and wench it tight, back when they built it, eighteen ninety-whenever-it-was. But that's what Grampa spotted, up there in the tree, that ancient steel swivel clasp finally dangling there free when the old house came down. He couldn't help thinking how handy a device like that might be, to tie up a dog or maybe a calf, should the need ever arise. So, before anyone could say Bob's your uncle, he was halfway up that tree and soon dangling, precarious, over the freshly poured slab and the skeletal studs of the new place, trying to wrench that ancient steel free.

I remember watching, fascinated, as this crane lifted and lowered these huge triangular, ready-built rafters into place over the stud walls going up as crews of men I'd never seen before worked that day. They'd swing that big cable around, somebody would lash it on at the peak of another piece, and the crane would hoist it up and swing it in place. There were these other two men, running around on the tops of those boards busily hammering away as each new rafter landed, light as a pebble in beach sand, up there atop the studded-out walls, then they'd scurry up the studs and crossbeams, easy as if they were walking on a patch of ground, unlash the tie-down and send the crane and its cable off again, in search of another rafter. How they did all that board walking way up there, I'll never know. I tried it on a few scrap pieces, down on the ground, and I couldn't stay on. Still, I watched them all morning, transforming what could've been a parking lot or the beginnings to an outdoor basketball court into something that started looking more like a house with every piece that went up.

What happened exactly, or even how, I don't think anyone's clear on. I guess the guy at the crane controls might've misjudged his distance or something. Maybe he got tired.

Because rather than a pebble in sand, that next rafter went down a lot more like a truck hitting pavement. Bumper first. Then, the rest tipping—ka-*thud*-*THUD!*—finally, into place. I felt it in the ground, way over where I was by the barn. For the first time that entire day, even the board-walkers had to grab onto something. They said a few things I couldn't quite make out from where I was, flashed some sort of hand signals I didn't understand, but then righted themselves and started to go back to work. Before they could, though, another ruckus got going, back where they already finished. It was enough of a ruckus, even the board-walkers turned to see. I looked where they did, too, but with all the workers' cars scattered about, I couldn't see a thing from where I was. I was supposed to stay out of the way, play there in the shade by the barn. But whatever was over there seemed to be increasing in interest, judging by the board-walkers, who abandoned their work entirely now and just stood there, gawking.

So, I left my shady spot out there by the barn and snaked my way through the labyrinth of cars. Nobody was working right then anyhow, I figured. As I finally broke free of my metal maze, the first clearing I found, I saw Dad and one of the builder men, shirtless, lifting Grampa off the ground and running toward Dad's truck. Mom threw it in park and slid across the seat to get the door. All as Grampa bellowed this awful sound. I hardly recognized him. Dire pain'll do that, though. Then I saw his leg, hanging kinda strange, the builder's shirt tied to it, the whole thing turning red, everyone's face twisted with worry. I started to make a run for the truck, but before I could budge, Gramma popped out of nowhere and cut me off. "There's nothing for you over there," I remember her saying. Then she spun me around, grabbed my hand and led me away. I went with her, my neck twisted almost all the way around, and I saw Dad's truck flinging gravel as he sped away.

I couldn't help it then, either. I cried.

I spent most of the rest of that day stuck in the "house," not that there was a *house* anywhere on our place right then. I was in the travel trailer that Gramma and Grampa got used, second-hand, so they'd have a place to stay until the old house got razed and the new one got built. I don't know how many of you ever set foot in a travel trailer in the mid-1970s, especially one that's—shall we say, *broke in?*—but it's not a pleasant experience, I'll tell you that.

For starters, it stank something fierce. My eyes might've been watering when I got there, but now they burned, too. Somebody said a pipe had broken, and water got everywhere. You ask me, it smelled more like that entire construction crew had run through the place, peeing on everything in sight. Not only did it reek, but it got hot as an oven inside there during the day. Mind you, nobody had air conditioning back then. Far as I knew it didn't exist. In fact, I wouldn't even see an air conditioned classroom until I got to high school. Doubt the trailer even had one installed. You wanted to get cool, you opened a window. That's just the way it was. And, yeah, we were all a bit more acclimated to the heat back then. Of course, most of us had enough sense not to stand around in the sun for no apparent reason. But with about a billion trees all around, somehow somebody came up with the bright idea of parking said trailer in the barest, sunniest spot on the place.

Why they did it was no big mystery. Grampa sure didn't have RV hookups anyplace about, so he set that trailer close to where all the stuff was that he needed to hook up. And that's what he did, spending the least one possibly could to accomplish his goal. As far as Grampa was concerned, he'd've been just as content sleeping in the barn or the back of his truck and trekking out into the cornfield whenever nature called. Gramma insisted on more civility, though, so they got that stinking thing. And Grampa hooked it up, just like he said he would. He rigged the water up with hose clamps and an old garden hose. You could taste the diazinon with every swallow. For sewer, he hooked up a black PVC pipe and ran the endpoint way off in the pasture, where it dumped out on the ground. Lastly, he basically jammed in a wire to the main power throw to give the place juice. To his credit, Grampa typically shut it off any time the coffee percolator wasn't on, no doubt the safest option, considering his knowledge of all things electrical was zilch. And after the electric co-op hooked up everything to the well house when they came to pull the meter off the old place, putting the trailer right beside it just made sense, for better or worse.

Still, I tend to think its placement might've been rethought a bit, if they'd known sooner that the windows down one whole side didn't work at all. You've probably seen ones like them someplace before. They had several individual slats of glass, that folded open and closed, kinda like how Venetian blinds work. You opened and closed them by turning this little crank. Seems the previous owners, though, broke all those little handles off, down that entire side of the old trailer. Way it was placed, that side was the only one that stood half a chance of catching the steady breeze I mentioned before. To give them credit, it probably wasn't their fault, the previous owners, that is. I couldn't come within three feet of those things, without them grabbing my shirt or catching a pant-loop. Small as I was, those little aluminum handles would yank me back, clean off my feet. Same thing happened to an adult, though, that aluminum crank snapped right off. Considering the design of that trailer forced everyone to walk right along that wall, that they were broken was no big shock.

Didn't help ease tempers much when Grampa made that discovery the night *after* he'd hooked everything up. Bet that would've been a night for vocabulary books, too. Considering it was Grampa, though, I'm sure most of it was in Czech.

Now if you had the right set of pliers, a baboon's grip, and caught that broken-off nub just so, you *could* wrench the window open. In about a half hour. And that's what he did, spending the least amount of time one possibly could to accomplish his goal. It helped ease some of the heat during the day and made it nice at night. Sometime, though, a heat shower sprang up. Now, it took equally long to wrench each of those windows back shut, by which time that nasty brown carpet got even nastier and browner, all sopping wet once again, which made that stench even worse.

But that's exactly where my sniveling butt got shoved, inside that awful, hot, stinking trailer, until Mom showed back up. I pitched a fit for a while, but after Gramma gave me the what-for about all the racket—she could get downright scary when she wanted to—I wound up just sobbing, silent, and sniffing at lot. Of course, there's only so much sniffing one can do when air smells like a rotten armpits. Plus, it was too damn hot for hysterics, and stifling a fit with nobody watching is a lot of unnecessary work. Mom showed back up, nine hours or six minutes later, it's kinda hard to tell when you're four. Felt like I'd died a thousand times from the heat, that old-trailer stench, and sheer boredom. Although I listened, attentive, through those paper-thin walls as she gave Gramma the news, wouldn't you know it? Most of it was in Czech.

No one was quite sure which came first, Grampa's fall from that tree, or the crane operator's boo-boo with the rafter. Considering we'd all felt it—that earth-shaking *THUD!*—most of the family was convinced the percussion knocked Grampa out of the tree. A few weeks later, though, I overheard some of the workers talking. They said the crane man had seen Grampa falling, and that's why he banged that rafter around like he did. He wouldn't've made a mistake like that unless he was distracted, they said, and you could tell by *how* they said it, they believed every word was the God's honest truth.

It's hard to tell sometimes whose truth to believe.

Either way, that fall left Grampa with a shattered leg, I eventually learned. A compound fracture in three places, the bone in his thigh had punched through his artery, and the impact of it all dislocated his hip, to boot. Left him in a thigh-high, heavy plaster cast, and confined to bed for six months straight while the bones mended, the family's hereditary arthritis slowly gnawing away at his back the entire time. Even when the doctor finally let him go back home with a cast half as tall, he was so stove up, he could hardly move for weeks afterward.

That very second, however—there in the truck bed with me—Grampa looked about nineteen again when Mom finally gunned the engine to life and got that old truck to move. He popped his hand on top of the cab a few times and let out a loud hoot, a big smile painted across his face. He had swagger written all over him, and he was just standing there, not a care in the world because he *knew*, without a doubt, he was about to *do* something most folks never dared. Sure, you might hear about such things, time to time, but usually, somebody somewhere embellished something along the way.

Not Grampa. He didn't have to. He was the real thing.

He spun around, then, to check his twenty-two. He worked the bolt and slide, made sure it was loaded, and eyed down its barrel to make sure it was still reasonably straight. He went back to relaxed then, leaned his back into the cab, and peered down at me. He could've been grabbing drinks someplace. All he needed was *studené pivo*. Can we get a *pivo prosím?*[6] That, and for the hay to stop swirling up in his face. But you can't have everything, as he often said. Despite a solid take off, Mom still ground her way through every gear

---

6   Czech, once again, as such: All he needed was a *cold beer*. Can we get a *beer please?*

on that three-on-the-tree '65 Chevy of his. When she finally found it, though, we hit speeds I'd never seen on that patch of dirt, Grampa hooting *rychleji, rychleji*,[7] the faster she went.

Odd as it sounds now, *I* normally drove for feedings on Friday evenings. Gramma was usually gone or leaving to her job at the nursing home, by then. Uncle Leon came and helped sometimes, but most of the time, it was just Grampa and me. Now I could pitch hay with the best of them—I could even load the bales back there, all by myself, despite the fact they outweighed me—Grampa taught me how to roll them up my body in one smooth motion so that I never actually bore any weight except for that initial yank. Still, Grampa worried about me falling out the back and getting trampled by the cattle. With good cause, too. A couple of those momma cows didn't like me at all, and the bull he had, Pepper, a smoky white brahman with black flecks all over him, he hated *everybody*. So, rather than have me back there with the cows, he decided one day, it was probably better if I drove.

Don't worry, nobody believed me back then, either.

When it came to driving, I had to stand the whole time, just to see over the dash, and just barely, at that. Wasn't bad as it sounds, though. Driving, for me, was more of a glorified roll, really. The brake and the clutch were the only pedals I ever used, and almost never at the same time. Even then, whenever I drove, Grampa was forever hollering at me. *Pomalé, pomalé*,[8] he'd say, which always made me hungry when he said it, me thinking of those tasty morsels wrapped in corn shucks that we always ate around Christmas time. We would've rolled backwards if I moved any slower, I thought most days, but I'd hit the brake, just the same, whenever I heard his voice. Be my luck, he fell out somewhere and I'd have to figure out how to shut that damn truck off by

---

7 Czech for *Faster, faster!*

8 Czech for *slow, slow!*

myself, which wasn't near as simple as you might think. He hadn't used a key in that ignition . . . well, ever, as far as I knew. There was a magic sequence he followed, between the choke and some other switch, hidden beneath the dash that he wouldn't tell me about for years. Yet here he was, hollering at Mom to give it more gas when she was already moving twenty times faster than I'd ever get that old truck to go.

At least I could put it in gear without all the noise.

Still, it was a definite departure from our regular routine, that's for sure. In fact, this was something altogether new. Mom usually dropped me off at Grampa's welding job in town. Then, she'd finish her ride home. Mom and I went to the same school, you see. She taught eighth grade science; I was in first grade, discovering all the ways I could get my knuckles whacked by that damn dowel-rod toting nun who taught my class. So, I spent lots of time riding shotgun with her, usually getting the what-for on whatever that sadistic nun told her before we left that day. Why Mom was there at the farm that exact day, I couldn't tell you. Memory overlaps itself sometimes. All I really remember about right then—aside from what was *about* to happen—was that old truck picking up speed across that gopher-pocked pasture. It rattled my every bone and tooth. Grampa, though, was still standing there, cool as Fonzie, that beat-up twenty-two rifle hanging loosie-goosey by his hip.

Seeing me getting jarred around good, he asked the obligatory, "You OK?" I bobbed my face up and down, hard as I could, so he'd know it was my answer and not just my neck giving out. Truth was, I hadn't had that much fun on the farm in . . . well, forever. Gramma, our resident safety monitor, would've gone off like a firetruck if she caught wind of any of this.

As if he heard my thoughts, Grampa glanced back at the house, then leaned forward and shouted out some new directions, ones that would put some trees between us and the kitchen window where we'd seen her last. Mom used her whole body on that big steering wheel. A tiny woman her whole life, she rarely did much of anything *manual* anymore. That old Chevy, however, was manual *everything*. She normally drove these luxury land yachts everywhere—Ford LTDs, Lincoln Towncars, Mercury Grand Marquis—think circa 1980, back when you could host a dance on the car hood, if you had to. They might need a full city block to turn around, but they practically drove for you. That's what the car salesmen always said, anyway. And Dad was big on driving nice cars and keeping them showroom polished. Grampa was a lot like that beat-up old gun of his when it came to cars. He drove their wheels off and was absolutely convinced washing one would only rust it out.

Me: I didn't care, myself. All I knew was this: Those behemoth cars sure weren't cool, not when other kids rode to school in Trans Ams, Camaros, Challengers, Mustangs, GTOs and Corvettes. Having grown up during one of the coolest car eras, ever, with my folks getting a new ride every couple of years, it seemed, they sure picked some butt ugly cars to put in our driveway. Things looked like they belonged out behind the funeral parlor. Only thing I liked about them was that I could stretch out on the back seat—arms, legs, everything—as far as I could reach, and never touch opposing doors at the same time until I hit junior high.

I'm sure we were doing all of twenty miles per hour across that pasture, maybe twenty-five, at best, but it felt like we were about to blast back in time, break the sound barrier or something. Still, Grampa's relaxed as he could be. Then, all at once, he spun, leaned his weight on the cab, and sighted down his barrel at whatever started this whole goose chase in the first place.

I looked where he's aimed, but I didn't see a thing. A buzzard, maybe, way up in the sky. But I couldn't tell. All I know is the faster we went, the more that old truck bucked me around. We could've been chasing a runaway rhino for all I knew; I was all about hanging on, just then. Still, I had pretty good eyesight back then. Surely some buzzard wasn't what all this was about, right? I mean, we had a whole pasture of them, a couple months back, after we butchered that steer and hauled the innards off to the woods. He could've shot the hell out of them then, and we wouldn't 've needed to bounce all around like this. That didn't seem right either, though. Grampa made a point of telling me how buzzards helped clean up our trash. Surely, we weren't chasing one of them, right? Or were we? I just couldn't tell.

I didn't know it then, either, but Grampa would teach me to shoot, using that very gun. The Fehrenkampf gun, I always heard it called. I always thought that Fehrenkampf was a *type* of gun, like an Uzi or Kalashnikov. Grampa set me straight, though, about the same time he taught me to shoot it. But more on that in a minute.

First, you've got to understand, Dad and Grampa had *several* guns between them. A dozen or more, each. Most were these gorgeous, highly-polished, finely-crafted works of art. They lived in fine cases, had these massive, powerful scopes, and glistening wood stocks, every part of them fragrant with this special shiny oil that Dad kept in this ornate case full of equally fascinating gizmos and thingamabobs for curious little boys. Every time he brought out such stuff, though, I got sent to my room. Don't know if Mom was worried Dad might not be as adept at this whole firearms thing as he let on, or if she was worried I'd become the next Lee Harvey Oswald or Charles Whitman. Regardless, Dad's and Grampa's guns were the kinds of things folks kept behind glass and dusted with only the softest rags. Anything less was criminal.

That Fehrenkampf gun was nothing like those guns. Not in the slightest. I said it lived in that back window of the truck, right? Well, Grampa *never* locked that truck, and it had to rain mighty damn hard for him to roll up a window.

But he took that truck everywhere—to town for haircuts, steel posts and wire, livestock sales, church, to work every day, and to the beer joints after—still, nobody ever took that rifle, even though it sat there right out in the open. Say what you will about how honest people once were. I think most folks left it there out of pity because it was plumb ugly. A tool, plain and simple. Like a hammer, 'cept I've seen nicer hammers. But because it was always handy, it also meant Grampa used it most. The only time I ever saw any of those other guns was when Dad and Grampa left for deer camp each year.

I remember shelling sacks of field corn, using these old hand-crank, cast-iron tools that probably predated every world war ever fought. I worked hard, too, through the hottest months of the year, filling sack after sack with corn in hopes that I'd get to go with them for a change. It'd be just us *men*, doing whatever it was that *men* do when they head off to the woods with an arsenal that could be on display at the Smithsonian.

Each year was the same, though. "Next year, we promise." Always, next year.

I needed to get bigger, stronger and, though neither ever said so, I'm sure they thought it really loud: Above all, son, you need to learn how to be *QUIET!* I remember them coming back laughing and carrying on. They'd start these stories and barely say five words before the other was doubled over laughing. They'd have these great hunting tales that began something like *I was about to call it a day when all the sudden, there he comes, right out of nowhere . . .* They'd talk about how they ate like kings and played dominos to all hours every night.

I liked dominos. I was pretty good, even . . .

When I finally got to go—I think it was corn sack nine thousand, seven hundred twelve that finally won them over, but who's counting?—Dad couldn't go. He had to work.

But aside from me nearly freezing my ass off, there were a whole lot of other traditions that didn't come to pass that year either. For starters, no dominos were played. They were *too noisy*, I got told. Nor were there any flame-kissed feasts. Not even close. We ate Spam, straight out of the can, congealed slime and all. And we certainly weren't staying up all night. No sooner than Grampa got back from his stand and downed his Spam, he was off to bed. He had to, if he was going back out at two past midnight or whenever it was he went stumbling off in the dark to avoid sunup by a good four hours. I wound up spending my whole time there bored out of my mind, afraid to fart because it might scare off a deer.

I just wasn't any good at all that *man* stuff, I guess.

My folks didn't let me do lots of things, but chief among them was learn too much Czech. Never mind that they spoke it all the time themselves, even asking me questions in the language I couldn't answer. Mostly, I think they used it, around me especially, so they could be sneaky. How do I mean? I remember with my own children, me and my ex-wife, not having a common shared language like Czech or French or Laotian (or English, most days, hence the *ex*-factor). Hell, anything would work, but since we didn't have an official language, we had to come up with something else for those ultra-secret parent talks. So, we spelled things out. That works exceptionally well if you're hoping your kids become national spelling bee champions. Try it sometime. If, by second grade, they aren't snagging stray words—like I-C-E-C-R-E-A-M, for example, or full-on correcting your screwed-up spelling from the backseat, rolling their eyes, and breaking off into multi-paragraphed compositions amongst themselves, complete with snarky side commentaries, all also spelled out, with regular emojis tossed in as well—you're not doing it right.

But that's how *I* learned what little Czech I know. Pure, unadulterated disobedience.

I'd pick up a phrase or two on my own, maybe even ask others who I knew spoke the language. But never with my folks' blessing. Never with their help. Why? Nine times out of ten, I think, so they could talk over my head. Seen and not heard, I was supposed to be.

I think even you, dear reader, knew how well that was going to work. You might already realize how frustrated I get when I'm not understood. If not, you might want to reread that first story. It's probably nine times worse when it's me who doesn't understand something because if I've learned anything in my years on this planet, it's that I can fix the latter. Not knowing it when it could be useful is just me being unprepared.

Besides, who wouldn't appreciate a heads up on any of these: Wanna stop for ice cream when we get to town?[9] Where did you put his gifts?[10] or I'm ready to yank his pants down and beat him, bare-assed, right here in front of the whole school![11]

Still, many from my generation never learned our family's native tongues, I don't care if they came from Mexico, Poland, Germany, France, Italy, or like mine, Moravia. Wait, *what?* That's right. There was no Czechoslovakia or Czech Republic when my family came here. When we left the Old World, almost all of Europe was part of Austria. Moravia was little more than a region—sort of like "the Hill Country" here in Texas or "Napa Valley" in California—but we're all part of the United States. I know the geo-political purists will

---

Should any of you ever find yourself in a similar position, the Czech would be:

9 *Chceš zastavit na zmrzlinu, až se dostaneme do města?*

10 *Kde jsi schovala jeho dary?*

11 And most important: *Jsem asi připravena vytrhnout si kalhoty tady a porazit ho holé-zadkem před celou školu!* I suggest running like hell if that last one should arise in conversation because you done pissed off somebody something awful. Beats the hell out of the alternative, anyway.

drop dead, me putting it like this, but one could liken that same analogy to the Old World, back when my people left it. If, that is, you don't mind comparing democracies to oligarchies, states to nations, and regional attractions to kingdoms and principalities. But they were all part of Austria, back then. If you remember your history, the immediate cause of World War I was the assassination of Archduke Franz Ferdinand and his wife, both of Austria (Kelly 2018). And while some elected folk would lead us to believe terrorists are a new deal of some sort, that assassination back in June 1914 was directly attributed to a Serbian-nationalist terrorist group.[12]

I remember as a boy hearing Czech spoken everywhere we went. There were Czech language radio stations, up and down the AM dial. Hallettsville, small as it has always been, had thirteen newspapers published there just a hundred years ago. More than half of them in languages other than English; five of them, Czech.

None exist today. Not those Czech radio stations, nor the Czech papers.

Fact is, I grew up in a heavily Czech area. I heard the language all the time as a kid. I still can today, if I hit the right

12 Martin Kelly, "Five Key Causes of World War I," (ThoughtCo.com., 2018). In June 1914, a Serbian-nationalist terrorist group called the Black Hand sent groups to assassinate the Archduke. Their first attempt failed when a driver avoided a grenade thrown at their car. Later that day, however, a Serbian nationalist named Gavrilo Princip assassinated the Archduke and his pregnant wife while they were in Sarajevo, Bosnia, which was also part of Austria-Hungary back then. Reportedly, the killings were committed in protest to Austria-Hungary having control of this region. (Kelly, *The Life and Death of Archduke Franz Ferdinand* 2018) Serbia wanted to take over Bosnia and Herzegovina. This assassination led to Austria-Hungary declaring war on Serbia. Russia then mobilized because of its alliance with Serbia, and Germany declared war on Russia because of a similar pact. On and on it went, one mutual defense alliance giving way to another until it was quite literally a worldwide war. The assassin, Princip, wasn't yet 20 when he committed the murders, which spared him from execution. Still, he died in prison just four years later from tuberculosis. Interesting, I thought, was the fact that today, a hundred years later, this area remains torn by war and constant unrest.

places. But with no one really learning it anymore, I suspect they, too, will likely join those radio stations and newspapers soon. Pick any town from around there, I dare you, find any school and the Czechiest surnames among that school's students. I bet anything you'll find twice as many kids there who can count one through to five in Spanish and almost none who can do the same in the only language their grandfathers spoke. My great-grandfather would be appalled.

All of us in that '65 Chevy did our part to keep Czech culture alive and well. My two elders were both native Czech-speakers. Both played in traditional Czech bands. I had more of an outlaw approach to my cultural cohesion, but that's how I do things, most days. I don't think my dutiful disobedience was all in vain, either. Sure, it served me well through the years, like helping know when that next ice cream stop might be or where my Christmas presents might be hidden or, best of all, when I needed to haul ass because I'd gotten on someone's last damn nerve. Hopefully, that's not all I accomplished, though. Who knows? What you hold in your hands could that last cry *Svoboda!*[13] behind which we can all rally, reclaiming what was once ours. I doubt it, but it worked for Mel Gibson in *Braveheart*. Still, I never dreamt I'd see a day when an entire culture—especially one as vibrant and accomplished as mine—would somehow fizzle and disappear as much as it already has. Not in just one lifetime, not one as brief and meaningless as mine, anyway. But if this is the last shot over the proverbial bow, our final alarm bell sounding before that once-thriving Texas treasure finally goes down, know this: I tried, at least.

---

13 Czech for *Freedom!*, which happens to also be the original name that was the original publication behind what became known as the El Campo Leader-News, which as the moniker suggests with its hyphenated title, is the melding of multiple publications into one, the last paper standing, so to speak. Svoboda, originally published entirely in Czech, fell to a lone to single section of the paper, by the mid-Twentieth Century, by the 1980s, a mere page, and by the 1990's, gone. It exists now only in archives and memories of a rebel few who dare not fade silent away.

You're reading my book.
What did *you* do?

Talk about a bunch of *zkažený* snakes, *Černá* cheats, and *falešný* philos'phers . . . I believe Grampa was right, when it comes to politics.

But we had business afoot, Grampa, Mom and me, bouncing across that pasture. It seemed what the old man spotted earlier, what set this whole story in motion and got him grabbing that beat-up Fehrenkampf gun, was his sighting of what we called on the farm your common chicken hawk. *Kuřecí jestřáb.*[14]

Technically, though, there's no such thing.

Oh, hawks will kill a chicken in a heartbeat. I've watched it happen. That part's scary real. But the name, that designation, *chicken hawk*, there's no such thing. Rather, it's what ornithologists call an "unofficial designation," in this case, a name frequently applied to three distinct species of North American hawks in the family *Accipitridae:* the Cooper's hawk, the sharp-shinned hawk, and the red-tailed hawk.[15] Although the Cooper's and sharp-shinned hawks may attack other birds, chickens do not make up a significant part of their diets. Red-tailed hawks, the largest of the three, have varied diets, and may opportunistically hunt free-range poultry (Lockwood 2016). Given its sheer size, I'd have to say this was a red-tailed hawk—a pterodactyl of one, actually—its

---

14 Czech for *chicken hawk.*

15 Mark W. Lockwood, *Field Guide to Birds of Texas,* (New York: Scoot & Nix, 2016). The unofficial names of other raptors derived from their supposed prey include the duck hawk (peregrine falcon), sparrow hawk (American kestrel), pigeon hawk (merlin), fish hawk (osprey) and quail hawk (Cooper's hawk).

wingspan covered the width of the pickup bed, as I recall. My own wingspan didn't do that. Not then, anyway.

Just to make sure we're all still following along: Mom was driving at warp speed (or twenty; it's kind of hard to tell and bumpy as hell), and Grampa just hollered up at Mom to change course. And I, in fact, did spot what Grampa was after—I only mistook that little speck in the sky for a high-flying buzzard—it's actually (or not actually) a chicken hawk. And just so we're on the up and up, killing birds of prey is entirely illegal. I wouldn't suggest repeating what you see here for any number of reasons, not least of which is that you'll wind up in jail.

And let's not forget that old gun of Grampa's—the Fehrenkampf gun, I always heard it called—the one that lived on the window gun rack of his truck. It looked like it had been dipped in seawater and left to dry in the August sun. For a decade. Maybe more. Its metal was nicked and dinged, beat to hell, really. I found a hatchet like that once, down some forgotten path through the woods that some camper left behind many moons (and monsoons) ago. It had oxidized itself to the stump it had been driven into. Looked like what somebody did to this rifle, a damn long time ago, all the way down to slamming it into the stump.

Fehrenkampf was the name of Grampa's old employer. He ran a feedmill, I think it was, out near the edge of town. Grampa worked there for decades—since before Mom was born to after she came home from college—Grampa even lost part of a finger working there, the tip of his ring finger (his ring lived on a nail by his bed any time he worked from that point onward). I hear he finished out his time with ol' Fehrenkampf, driving this old bobtail truck, delivering feed-stuffs from Hallettsville to La Grange, way back when. For some reason, Old Man Fehrenkampf (I never knew his first name) took a shine to Grandpa. Not hard to imagine. I was certain Grampa was responsible for lighting the heavens each night, just so he could tell me about constellations.

Old Man Fehrenkampf gave that gun to my Grampa one day, I heard. It may not have looked like much, but in Grampa's hand, it was a lethal weapon. He'd never been a soldier or anything. Army said he had flat feet or some such, so he never joined his brothers to fight the Germans or Japanese. Uncle Blase survived it OK, but he lost a couple other brothers in that war. A couple more came back, but in body only. Not much more. Not the fun-loving boys Grampa told me about as he pointed out the stars. Why Old Man Fehrenkampf gave a gun to an employee who chopped off part of his hand working at his place of business, I never figured out. But he did. And despite outward appearances, that gun was one of Grampa's most prized possessions. Watching him cradle it in his arms then, you'd swear it was encrusted in diamonds.

Not to interrupt this trip down Memory Lane, but remember that new route he pointed Mom toward? Well, only Grampa knew this, then, but do the words *blind ravine* mean anything to you? Well, we were aimed right at one and *gaining* speed.

Where's our Dixie horn when we need it?

And you know how sometimes, when things get truly bizarre, how time seems to slow-motion on you? Like when the sound went all funny and the Six Million Dollar Man would leap up a three-story building or chase down a semi in the 1970s TV series. No? Well, how about Neo in the *Matrix*? Well, that's exactly what happened! Maybe not *exactly*, exactly. Nobody stopped any bullets with his bare hand or saved the entire world as he knew it. A chicken or two, maybe, but hardly *all* of society.

Everything else was pretty much the same, though. I watched as Grampa kinda hunkered down, right when Mom topped that ravine, it turned out. All at once, he launched straight up. Like Superman up. He didn't hardly move a muscle, but he was suddenly flying. All he needed was a cape. I couldn't believe what I was seeing. Before I could really wrap my head around that, though, the truck bed shot me up in the air like it suddenly went trampoline beneath me. I'm not kidding! And because I tried to fight it and hang on, I went up ugly. Nothing at all like the grace and poetry of motion that was Grampa's sudden gift of flight. Ugly or otherwise, I was weightless, floating.

Right about then, too, as I'm kind of rolling there in the sky, I look down below me, below the truck. That's when I learned what a "blind ravine" was as I watch, there in flight, as Mom pulls of this perfect, Duke-boy, car jump. I'm talking full-on, *the bridge is out, Bo, and Sheriff Roscoe P. Coltrane's hot on your tail,* launch of a truck that looks more like Cletus' or Uncle Jesse's than anything Bo or Luke Duke ever drove. Still, Mom pulled it off like champ. You go, Mom! *YeeeeHAAAWWW!*

I looked back at Grampa, and he was still flying like he knew what he was doing. One minute, he looks something akin to Iron Man, soaring through the sky. The next, he was in full sniper mode, looking like went prone, flat on his belly, but as best I could tell, he was as nearly vertical, straight up and down, as a fellow could get. But what did I know? I start to spin slowly round again. I could feel my stomach starting to knot up on me. Grampa looked still as post over there in his flight space. He continued sighting, and finally put a finger on the trigger. He took a breath, blew it out, and pulled. I didn't even hear it, just saw the barrel's white puff, and almost immediately, he started floating back down again. I had no such luck. I was pretty sure I might be stuck there, forever, doomed to this permanent spin cycle until I barfed my guts up. Having made an entire revolution up there, I found Grampa again. He landed right where I'd been standing earlier, beside the tailgate, soft as a pebble in sand. I can't help but think he must've practiced this whole thing before at some point. What I can't wrap my head around, though, is how?

I felt gravity start tugging on me, too, and begin my awful descent. I must've looked half asleep, coming down, my eyeballs fighting—desperately—to slam shut, yet at the same time, stay open long enough to know which side of my body was about to be mauled. Somehow, I drifted off course—must've been all the spinning—best I could tell, I was aimed straight for the fender and siderail. Oh man, this was gonna hurt . . .

If something like that's coming and there's nothing you can do about it, what do you do? Would you wilt and go limp, or tighten every muscle, go stiff as a board? I couldn't decide. But it sure was going through my mind. Grampa'd know what to do. Maybe not, but he sure looked like he'd done it before. I still hadn't figured out how, though . . . oh man, this was gonna hurt.

Thankfully, my body decided what I should do for me. No, I didn't *puke*, though I'm afraid I was a hellova lot closer than I maybe wanted to admit. No, I went rigid as one of my Star Wars action figures. Guess it came from those repressed memories I had from me and my neighbor, Joey, launching them way up in the sky one day on these rockets he had. He'd tape them on with this real sticky black tape. He even used *real* matches to light the fuses. He was a couple years older than me and got to ride his bike around out in the street whenever he wanted. Even at night. I thought he was so cool . . .

What we learned, though, was that Star Wars people—the poor kneeless, stiff-armed bastards—held up surprisingly well under rocket power. G.I. Joe action figures, with their bendable extremities, typically lost something *en route*. We couldn't make out if it was happening when the rocket exploded, way up in the sky or if his limb loss occurred at the point of impact on the return. So, we sent the same fellow up several times in a row until there was nothing left but a head and a half-burned torso. Ol' Joey, so ready to send him up so many times in a row, too. I should've known something was up.

"What the *hell* are y'all doing?" Mom screamed at our backs.

She stood there, arms crossed, hip jutted; her jaw locked—face red and getting redder—straight angry, all over her. Judging from the way the grass was mashed down under where she stood, she'd been there a while already. No telling how many launches she'd witnessed, us ruining his toys, especially the G.I. Joe I held in my palm. I was going to look like him when she was done with me.

With no way out, I flashed my terrified eyes at my older, cooler friend.

He's calm as anything. *Phew*, I recall thinking. He knows what to do. He's fielding this.

"Hello, Missus H," he said, even flashed a genuine smile.

Polite. Formal. Pleasant even. Man, he's good. We might make it out of this just yet . . .

"My dad gave me some rockets as a birthday gift last week," he said. "I was just showing them to ol' Bobbo here."

Mom hadn't budged and still looked mad as hell, but I couldn't care less. He called me *Bobbo!* He gave *me* a nickname—I never had one of *those*—none I wanted anybody repeating, anyway. He even reached over when he said it and mussed my hair. We really *are* friends. Man, he's *so* cool. That time I thought he sic'd his dog on me when I got off the bus, clearly that must've been some awful misunder—

"It was all *his* idea to tape *HIS* action figures to them," he added, his usual bully meanness flashing back to his face with every *his* he uttered, his big fat lip curling into a smirk.

As his words slowly sank in, I spotted *my* Star Wars case, down there by his feet, all but two of them now scattered *somewhere* down the street. It was then, too, I realized that the stump of the G.I. Joe action*less* figure I held in my hand—the one with no more than a head and a charbroiled torso—was the one and only G.I. Joe that I had.

I couldn't help myself. Those tears came out of nowhere. They streaked both my cheeks.

"You're such a chump!" he heckled, tossed the black roll of tape at me, turned his back and ran off, laughing. And damn the luck if that tape he tossed didn't hit me in the eye. I stood there completely defeated and still had Mom to deal with. I never found all my Star Wars people, and poor G.I. Joe went up on her shelf to show Dad what I done, and later every relative who might get me a replacement. Never heard the end of that one. Never got another action figure ever again, neither.

I guess if there's anything good to come out of that awful story, it's this: Somehow my body remembered it all right then and went stiff as a board. No knees or elbows here, bub . . .

As I braced for the impact and felt those tears coming again, I was still fighting my eyeballs to keep them from clamping shut as I watched, scared as hell, the fender getting closer. Then, like he wasn't even trying hard, Grampa kicked apart the hay bale between him and me and reached out—one-armed, his rifle's still in the other—and snagged me out of the air. Didn't even look like he was paying attention, he did it so nonchalant. He set me down in the bed, right about the time Mom slammed on the brakes and sent us flying toward the cab. She climbed out of that truck with eyelids so open it's amazing the ball part didn't roll right out.

On the plus side, the look was for the Duke Boy-jump she'd pulled off, unwitting and unwilling. She totally missed all the Rocketman antics in the back. Before she could utter a word, Czech or otherwise, all sorts of racket broke out, directly behind her—limbs cracking, branches popping, twigs snapping—and a solid, resounding *THUD!* Something heavy hit the ground hard.

Grampa was back to Duke Boy, leap-sliding over the siderail, charging toward whatever hit like he was part Brahman bull. I scrambled for the open tailgate myself, trying to catch up. Poor Mom had spun all the way around in a complete circle. I can't imagine what all that must've sounded like to her, right behind her, down there at ground level. Grampa poked at something on the ground a couple times with the barrel of that Fehrenkampf gun, then bent down and scooped up the source of the racket— a big goddam hawk—it might've seemed like a speck, way up in the sky, but it was huge up close, bigger than me. Did a hellova number to the tree it crashed into, but the only real wound on it was what looked like a pinhole, right in its breast.

I'd just seen my Grampa fly in the sky like some redneck superhero, fire just one shot and nail that enormous chicken-eating bird right in the heart. He couldn't have done it better if his name was Cupid. I've never seen anything like it, before or hence.

Not by a long shot. I doubt I ever will . . .

THE LEGEND OF CHUNK

August is just about the best month of the whole year, I've always thought. Some may say I've got it all wrong. June's a better pick, at summer's start, when everything is still new. Maybe, but most kids, I think, get so giddy about the schoolyear ending and the exponential possibilities of summer ahead, they waste most of their first month. They sleep half a day that first week because they can, then spend the next couple weeks just finding their groove. And after all the family vacations, extended stays with relatives, and assorted camps and such, that first month's long gone and lost in no time. Besides, the mindset's all wrong in June. Folks are like, "Who cares if we don't do it today? We still got all summer, *right?*"

Not so in August. Even as kids, you sense its mortality. By then, you're full-on summer grooving. None of that amateur crap like in June. At the same time, however, you know your days are numbered. You want to make everything count, milk the most of every moment. It wasn't something we talked about—not if we could avoid it, anyhow—but always, as soon as the calendar flipped the page on July, you'd feel it, right there on the shadowy edge of everything, a stark realization that it's all nearly done. Summer's almost gone. Makes you a bit more adventurous, a bit more courageous, a bit—well—just *MORE!*

I've never seen anyone better embody that sense of *more-ness* than my old buddy Chunk. He lived a couple houses down, back where we used to live before my folks moved to different towns. Even today still, whenever I picture my childhood, my head turns to those golden afternoons spent in the shade of the giant sycamores that lined the length of Fairview Avenue, the cicadas unwinding their crazy metal screech from their boughs as we pedaled by on our bikes. They were good times, just as free as the wind, most especially in August.

But for all the kids who lived on our street back then, nobody was quite like Chunk. If you never met him, you probably know his type. Kinda whiny. Clumsy. A ginger with milk white skin that never tans, and every inch of him, freckled. Every inch I cared to see was, anyway. Combine it all with a set of Coke-bottle eyeglasses, an inhaler he huffed whenever he got nervous, and a belt-size twice my dad's— a condition he always swore had something to do with his glands, even as he scarfed Butterfingers two at a time—and it's a wonder he ever made it to junior high. The kid just seemed to attract ridicule, and kids could be damn cruel. He just stayed the butt of everybody's jokes, practical or otherwise, like he had a target painted on him or maybe a big fat bully magnet in each pant pocket. That he wasn't straight miserable was something of a miracle. He seemed immune all the ribbing. Somehow, he just laughed it all off.

Believe me, Chunk was a vast improvement, as far as names go. His real name was Marion Mansfield Manersik IV, meaning his relatives saw fit to curse three male generations with a name like that before him. Had to feel for the guy.

But just ask anyone, Chunk became a legend beside the pool that day.

I remember our swimming instructor made us watch these films of Olympic divers as part of our lessons. They'd launch off platforms and twist, tumble, spin, flip—basically execute every manner of aerial acrobatics imaginable—and then, right before they touched water, they'd straighten back out somehow and break the water's surface like they could split molecules just by thinking hard.

Don't know if you ever tried diving into a pool *without* making a splash, but best we could tell, it was right next to impossible. None of us even came close. But a guy built like Chunk? Forget about it. So, if he was gonna splash anyway, Chunk figured he might as well learn to do it right. He spent hours watching some of the older boys who hung around and loved nothing more than dousing random passers-by with sheets of pool water. They could drench a full-grown man, head to toe, with any number of dives they'd perfected. They even had the coolest names for those dives, too, we all thought. Like the Flying Squirrel or the Can Opener, the Jackknife or, everybody's favorite, the tried-and-true Cannonball.

Chunk studied their every move, even asking questions, for several mornings in a row before he decided to try and apply what he learned one afternoon. Thus far, however, all his learning seemed for naught. Instead of landing anything that half-resembled a cannonball (knees tucked, butt striking the water first), Chunk kept rolling forward and—*SPLAT!*— some of the worst belly-flops you ever saw. Couldn't hardly watch without wincing as his pale skin smacked against that water like it was made of concrete. Just hearing it could bring a tear to your eye. I'm pretty sure the rest of us would've tossed in the towel long ago.

Not Chunk. No sir. The more he failed, the more determined he got.

So, after more belly flops than anyone could count, Chunk climbed back out to try again, his chest chapped raw with failure already. Even for guy like Chunk, you could tell it was starting to wear him down. Still, something about the way he stood up, set his jaw and whipped his head back to shake the pool from his hair made us certain that next attempt would be it. Something magical. The cannonball to end all cannonballs.

He backed up on his launching zone just as far as facilities would allow, the unforgiving metal diamonds of the hurricane fence enclosure pressing hard against his fleshy, freckled back. Face pinched in concentration, he gazed off someplace into the vast emptiness over the pool, visualizing the one sure way to accomplishment that only he could see, and there he stood for several seconds, statue still. His focus, unbreakable. I can't help but think that's got to be what David looked like as he sized up the mighty Goliath, staring with such powerful intensity, everyone there just knew that big bastard was done for.

Suddenly, Chunk lets loose this Jurassic, guttural growl as he shot forward with everything he had. Nearly every eye at the pool was on Chunk as he approached the water's edge. We barely breathed. Remarkably agile, built like he was, he ramped his speed with each new bound. Those of us rooting for him looked part pretzel, we were so twisted up, crossing every finger and toe we had because each of us knew, it was now or never.

He was moving full bore as he angled for the deep end and readied for that ever-critical foot plant, the final power-thrust up he would need to match what the older kids had pulled off all morning long, when—*FFffft!*—he slipped. The steely determined eye he wore a mere moment before gave way to pure terror, unbridled, as Chunk went flailing into the abyss, unable to pull back if you paid him. Time seemed to stop as he went suddenly airborne, nothing but plump, pasty white boy hanging midair, awkwardly suspended; trajectory, completely unknown. The rest of us must've sucked the air dry with our collective gasps.

Well, most of us did, anyhow.

Remember how I said that *NEARLY* every eye at the pool was on Chunk as he approached the water's edge? I suppose another way putting it might be that every eye but either of Samantha Summerly's was on Chunk as he approached the water's edge, which is an entirely accurate assessment of the situation as well. Almost poetic, really, when you consider she was so accustomed to having all eyes on her. She may have been a few years older than us, but we were all smitten. I know I was, anyway. And not surprising, I don't think. She's the first girl I'd ever seen in two-piece swimsuit. Like *ever*. And let's just say she was one of those types of girls that bikinis were made for. I do believe she had one for every day of the week, in a whole rainbow of colors. All I know is that I could hardly focus on much else, whenever I saw her wearing one.

Samantha arrived at the pool right as it opened, most every day during summer. She typically wore a large, white button-down shirt that, judging from its size, had to belong her dad or something because, in order to pull off wearing it, she had tie off the excess cloth across the bottom into a wide knot, just above her belly button, exposing that gorgeous golden tan she had, right at her midriff. She'd find one of those poolside lounge chairs, away from all us boys, and there she'd prep for her day at the pool, slowly sliding out of her street clothes—that big blousy white shirt and the tiniest Daisy Dukes you ever did see, barely larger than what they were covering up—to reveal whatever the day's color might happen to be, her perfectly manicured toenails always painted to a perfect match.

After that was when she began her daily oiling ritual, coating every inch of herself in a glistening radiance that smelled of coconuts and cinnamon. I get butterflies telling you about it, even today still. That typically took a good thirty minutes, every day, the way she did it, but I could've watched her for hours. Then, she'd dive in the pool, always the deepest part where few of us dared swim for any longer than we had to, and there she stay a while, elegantly treading the blue, shimmering waters, stroke after luscious stroke, before she'd climb back out, pat the excess water from her hair with a beach towel that matched whatever shade she might be wearing that day. Then she'd brush those dark brown locks of hers, the same way she swam, stroke after luscious stroke, clean past her bottom, which seemed to awaken each individual strand, leaving them dangling in tiny ringlets that had a life of their own to dance loosely over sun-kissed skin or toy at the edges of what little cloth she wore. Afterward, she'd board her inflatable lounger and spend the rest of her pool time working on that incredible tan of hers, floating wherever the waters carried her until sometime about midafternoon, just as the sun got its hottest. Then she'd climb out, make some adjustments to the suit she wore, collect her things, board her Jeep, and leave, always returning the day after to repeat the entire process over again.

She ignored us boys, most days. But there would be no ignoring Chunk. Not that day.

Chunk was headed right for her.

He tried everything—turning, spinning, twisting—he even kicked his legs and pumped his arms, up in the air—no use, though. If anything, what little movement he managed only better aligned her float with his landing zone. What's worse, despite his seeming to float, weightless, out there over the pool, gravity's tug began adding a definite down-ward motion to Chunks unexpected flight plan, a pull that increased with every second that ticked by.

He had just one trick left. With distance closing, Chunk sounded this blood-curdling shriek that hit octaves I've never heard equaled, prior nor hence. Startled, Samantha, belly down right then, rolled just in time to see this freckled blob closing fast. About half a second later, full body contact, and both sank out of sight, waters churning like they were set to full boil.

Had he not sounded like a ring wraith right then, I'm sure Chunk would've been proud. You should've seen the wall of water he displaced that day. It was truly something.

But that wasn't even the best part. Somehow in watery collision of slippery flesh, Samantha lost her top, a fact no one realized until Chunk finally surfaced, gasping for air and arms flailing, and there, perfectly perched on the top of his head like a set of Disneyland mouse ears might fit, were two perfect aquamarine cones. It took some longer than others for their minds to catch up to their eyeballs, but we all eventually arrived at the same conclusion. Namely, if Chunk was wearing her top like a tiara, guess where else it was probably not?

Samantha must've realized what happened early because she dove for bottom after Chunk knocked her off her float, and there she stayed, following the curved floor up the wall at the far side of the pool, as far away from us boys as she could get. She presently rested her chin on the backs of her hands, her forearms and the rest of her newly exposed front side pressed firmly to the pool's side wall. Nothing at all visible.

Chunk was the absolute last to realize what treasures he was inadvertently carrying. Even then, it took serious prompting from those of us at poolside. But he finally reached up and plucked his mock ears. You should've seen him as he cracked code on what, exactly, he held in his hands just then. His lightbulb eventually flickered on, but unlike the rest of us, hoping for an eyeful of boob, Chunk scanned the water—*serious*—looking worried. He told me later he was scared he hurt her. Finally, he spotted her on the pool's far side, clinging to the wall and looking especially helpless and small. Neither was a look common to her. Not the Samantha we all knew. All at once, just like those Olympic divers in the films, Chunk straightened himself and unleashed this sleek, fast, swimming machine that none of us had ever seen before. In no time flat, he closed the expanse between Samantha and him. He kept to her back, the perfect gentleman.

"I'm *soooo* sorry!" we heard him tell her, his voice, pleading and sincere.

What they said afterward was anyone's guess. Chunk

never shared. But after both said a few words back and forth, Samantha looked back our direction, her boobs still pressed to the side the pool, and smiled a delicious and devious grin.

"Go for it," we heard her tell Chunk.

He nearly swaggered as he bobbed his way our direction, smile clean ear to ear as he put some distance between him and Samantha. Then, with a swift and powerful kick, Chunk launched up, clean above his waist, and at the height of his thrust, he pumped his fist, Samantha's top, fluttering prize flag, and sounded his very best "*Woohoohoo!*"

We couldn't help ourselves. Chunk had earned a cheer from all of us that day.

And just like that, it was done. Dad and I left for another town not long after Chunk's big day at the pool. I wasn't thrilled about leaving my friends behind, but I wasn't about to let my dad wander off all alone, either. My younger brother and sister stayed with mom in the old neighborhood, but just for a while. They didn't even finish the entire schoolyear there. Turns out, none of us would know another summer like that one, free as the wind and not a care in the world. Not in my family, anyway. Mom and my siblings eventually moved way upstate after she married Jack, the college professor, and it wasn't long until Little Jack came along after. I'd visit them, time to time, and they us. But mom hated my brother and sister spending any more time than necessary in the city, and Dad hated making the daylong drive way up there. I eventually quit asking him to take me. Besides, I had school and a job, and later, college. Then I was off on my own. Wasn't like I really fit in up there, anyway. Toss a city rat like me out into the countryside—even one nice as theirs—and he'll almost always starve a little. No matter how many scenic mountains, crisp autumn mornings or quaint little farms down winding country paths there might be. Not fitting in eventually becomes the one thing you're truly good at, that far away from your element.

Likewise, I rarely saw any of my friends from the old neighborhood again after that summer either. Funny how you can go from practically being brothers with somebody, like we all were then, to not knowing if those same folks are even alive still. It happens, though. A whole lot more than most of us care to admit. Don't get me wrong, I still think fondly of them and the summers we shared, the way folks do, every now and again. But that's about it.

I did run into one of the old crew, a couple years back, outside this coffee shop in a part of the city I'd never been to before. Not that *old crew* really applied Tommy Sanderson. Most definitely applied to *Vito* Sanderson. Vito was the star athlete of our crew. You name the sport—I don't care what it was—and Vito'd be best at it, every time. I guarantee it. But Vito's mom used to insist we drag Tommy, Vito's kid brother, everywhere we went. He was more an annoyance than an actual crew member. Still, he was a somewhat familiar face in unfamiliar surroundings. Sort of. He spotted me, broke the ice, and dropped more than a few hints as to who he was. It took me a few tries to even come up with a name. Course, I've never been good at names.

Was kinda nice to hear about folks I grew up with, though. Would you believe that sweet Miss Samantha became Mrs. Marion IV? Seems ol' Chunk might've knocked more than her top off, that day at the pool. From what Tommy told me, they both still live there in the old neighborhood. They bought the house across the street from Chunk's parents after they both got out of college. Chunk's a school teacher, a swim coach, of all things. Samantha's an attorney. They've even got a whole pasal of kids themselves now, including a Marion V, from what Tommy said.

We didn't chat too long, me and Tommy. He asked about the folks, and me, his. And before long, we'd exhausted every inch of common ground he and I shared. He kept saying how we needed to stay in touch more, but when all was said done, we parted ways without even exchanging phone numbers.

That sort of thing happens a lot more than we care to admit, too.

Rather hard to believe, still. Me running into Tommy like that. Chunk hooking up with Samantha like he did. Or them being parents now and cursing yet another generation with that awful name. Maybe not so much hard to believe as it's a lot to take in all at once. Mostly, I guess, because we're all still kids ourselves, in my memories, always reliving that same summer, again and again, in constant loop. That's the thing about memories, though, why they remain memories, I suppose.

But I can't say I'd change them any either, my memories.

Chunk's probably a damn fine teacher and has taught legions of kids all about swimming and diving and who knows what else. I'm sure, too, his bride is an amazing lawyer and mother to their children. And I bet it would be a real hoot to see what they turned out like, and how much their kids probably favor one or the other, from how I remember them.

I still prefer my memory reels to all that, I think. They're familiar, comfortable, and in many ways, comforting. I mean, is picturing Samantha, hard at work in some law library, hair in a bun, working on some case, or with a baby on each hip and spit up on her blouse really the image you want floating around in your head as you drift off to sleep?

Call me crazy, but I'd still rather hear about the affable oaf who, quite literally, stumbled his way into something quite amazing one day with what we thought was the perfect poolside goddess, her tantalizing ringlets toying with the hems of her swimwear.

Why? Because how else could we wonder if—just perhaps—that buttery sweet scent of coconut doesn't still linger on the wind somewhere, whenever she's around? For everything else we have to deal with in this old life—waiting in line, annual colon cancer checks and the absolute mindless boredom that fills so much of our ordinary days—I sure hope it does, with just a dab of cinnamon, to spice it all up. It's that part of us, no matter how old we eventually get, that still imagines things, that still daydreams. Just seems to me what the good Lord had in mind for us, the day he uttered those four fateful words into the vast nothingness that came before it. "Let there be life." I mean, I can't think of a better reason he would've said something like that. Can you?

Roll Models

"You gotta let yourself get hit a few times so you can see it's not so bad, or so you can see how bad it really is." Those words somehow made perfect sense to Jesse, clutching his ratty old football on the practice field sidelines.

After all, his big brother Jake had said them, and when it came to football, Jake hung the moon, far as Jesse was concerned. He'd been the starting quarterback for four years now and a star athlete for as long as anyone could remember. No matter what he played, he always rose to the top—baseball, basketball, soccer, wrestling—but he truly shone on the football field. Jake's room was littered with trophies. When he was little, Jesse thought those gold and silver players posed at their tops actually *were* his brother. He so longed to be like him, to see that pride beam in everyone's faces when he walked by or hear the crowd chant *his* name. Just once, maybe. Just like Jake. Jesse would, too. Soon as he got big as Jake, he would. Of course, at fifty-two pounds at age eight, "big as Jake" was still a far-off dream.

"Now you gotta hold that ball tight, like *this*," Jake told him.

Jesse snugged the ball close, mimicking big brother's every move. The team's top star was giving *him* pointers. Wait 'til the boys in class heard about this!

He paid no mind to Jake's friends, drifting away, smirks on their faces.

"And you gotta crouch down low, like *this* . . ."

Jesse matched his stance.

"OK. You ready?"

Jesse nodded, determined.

"OK. I want you to run along this line. I'm gonna try and knock the ball out of your hands, understand?"

Jesse retightened his grip, focused.

"Alright, *GO!*"

Jesse sprinted ahead, fast as his knobby knees would carry him. *Finally!* It was *his* turn to shine, his turn to show his hero what *he* could do, instead of always the other way around. He focused on closing the gap between him and Jake. Had no idea the linebackers were closing in, one from each side.

Jesse's entire vision went white when they hit him, full on, sending him flying, face-first for the bleachers. His knee split open, chin, too, and his insides ached. Worse still, he had no idea where his ball was, nor did he care much.

He climbed back up on unsteady legs, trying not to cry.

He looked downfield for his brother, checking to see if he was OK.

That's when he spotted Jake and his friends, pointing, doubled over in laughter. Jesse couldn't stop his tears, which only made them laugh all the harder. He wasn't even the first kid *that day* they'd tricked into their depraved prank, he later learned.

His big brother never glowed with quite the same shine after that.

It was a shitty thing to think about as Jesse looked down at his brother's flag-draped casket.

My First Time

Where I was, what I was doing, what I had on (and later changed into), everything—I remember it all—because it was like nothing I'd known before, an experience like no other. Especially that first time. Part of me was terrified, flat mortified everyone would find out that I truly had no clue what I was doing. That they'd hate it, tell me I'd done it all wrong. Course, call me crazy. Sometimes there's an incredible thrill in that, too. The sheer challenge of it all as my inner risktaker demands more, pushes me ever farther. It enlivens the adventurer in me something fierce, let me tell you, and the public nature of it all uncovers this hidden voyeur I never knew existed. Keeps the adrenaline on constant tap, that's for sure, between the thrill of the chase and fear of being found out. I ain't gonna lie, part of me—if only just a smidge—was pretty sure I had it going on, at the same time. How else could you explain how very natural it all seemed to me. I just knew I had a knack, a talent, if you will. And I just knew I'd never get enough. I was driven, focused, forever thereafter on the hunt. It consumed me. Became my all. Who I was and ever wanted to be.

I should've known better, I guess. Like all good things, they end. Eventually. Been my experience, anyway. Why I thought this might be different, I doubt I'll ever fully explain. Because it wasn't. No matter how fun or fulfilling the ride might've been, it was simply gone one day. Vanquished. Decimated. Not even a fart on the wind to remember her by, I'm sad to say.

Unless you were one of us, the hangers-on, the candle

lighters for sweet yesterday. Bearers of a torch that, deep down, we all knew would never burn near as bright as before. Still, we held tight, just the same, because it's all we knew how to do. If I was to be truly good at just one thing, I always figured I sure as hell could've done far worse.

All I know is I've never been quite the same since.

Sure sign it was hellova first time, I guess. . . .

If what I describe wasn't embarrassing enough already, here's the final coffin nail. Would you believe it was the product of what they called the Political Science Club? That's what one of my school's teachers chose to call that loose conglomerate that formed among some of us nerdier, slacker types, anyway. I remember we hated the moniker, mostly because we had no idea what political science was. Sounded as fun as a getting a tooth yanked, having blood drawn, or spending an afternoon practicing long division. But having a name like that gave us a legitimate reason to loiter around his office each day after lunch. Other than play *Dungeons & Dragons*, that is, a pastime we'd all taken to with some tenacity at the time, as I recall. Lord knows we couldn't admit to such things out in public. Were it to get out I spent my afternoons roll-playing the part of an effeminate elf with tendency toward uncontrollable kleptomania who botched more magic than he ever got right and landed himself in the worst fixes because of his traits, there'd be no end to the harassment. It certainly wasn't scoring me any points with the ladies, in case you were curious. And given that our teacher suggested his club to us in an "or else" kind of way, what else were we going to do? So, we all signed on, happily or otherwise, most of us quietly planning to change that name at first opportunity.

Turns out, it was best thing we could've done. Made our clandestine D&D groups a lot simpler to solicit, anyway, especially in the lunch line in front of all those football jocks and diehard FFA types, who loved nothing more than trying to cure our weirdness with wedgies and wet willies. Just a, *Hey, you coming to the meeting?* A knowing nod, and we were on. If someone new came along, seriously into politics between ages twelve and fifteen, trust me, he wouldn't need much goading to get with the program. And, as if things could possibly get any better, tying ourselves to a legitimate academic subject landed us extracurricular funding from the school, which happened to arrive just a few weeks before the opening of Laurence Luckinbill's one-man show in Austin called *The Return of LBJ*.

We boys were far more familiar with L.A. Laker Magic Johnson or *Miami Vice's* Don Johnson than we would ever be with Lyndon Baines Johnson. I mean, we knew that last guy had been president—a few of us did, anyway—but he could have served somewhere between Washington and Lincoln for all we cared. Dude was ancient history, somebody our parents or grandparents might've liked. If they were really *old*, maybe. But why should we give half a shit about him? I mean, he never did anything for us, we were pretty sure, and certainly nothing from way back then could have any possible bearing on us, *right?*

Still, going to the show got us off campus for an evening, which for us, was priority *numero uno* every night of the week. It increased by a hundredfold our only true mission in life right then, too, which was, of course, to catch a glimpse of someone other than one of dudes running around in blown-out socks and tightie-whiteys for another fun-filled evening back at our dorm. Chances also increased exponentially that encounters with the opposite sex, however awkward those might be, might not involve somebody old enough to be our moms, like most of the female staffers were back at the ranch. Barring somebody's sister showing up for some unexpected family visit during the week, our chances of even seeing a girl were slim to no way in hell at our boys-only campus.

For all we didn't know about the subject of said play—ol' LBJ—we made up for in buckets with knowledge about the actor. One of his roles, anyway. It was big hit for a bunch of sci fi nerds like us. Luckinbill, you see, had starred in 1989's theatrical release of *Star Trek V: The Final Frontier* as Spock's half-brother Sybok. I'd already seen it twice, and it had only been out for a month. If Sybok was going to be in Austin in a few weeks, we were there. Even if he was playing some dead president we knew next to nothing about.

"You'll finally get the chance to rub elbows with Austin's high-society types," Turner, our teacher, told us. The play would be showing at Austin's historical Paramount Theatre, he explained, a far cry from the sticky-floored auditoriums we normally piled in to watch the latest out of Hollywood while we guzzled Pepsis by the gallon and stuffed fistfuls of popcorn and candy down our throats.

"This will be a completely different experience," he said. "You'll need to dress nice."

Our eyes glazed as we left him standing there. All this talk of attire and society matters meant less than the president bit. Plus, it was dull as hell. Why was he giving us all that grief, anyway? It wasn't like we'd never been out in public before. Besides, we'd all heard of "high society," so we knew it was thing. When it came to clothes, fine—we'll wear our new high-tops to the damn thing, if you insist—but that was it. We weren't about to put on airs for anyone. Can't be that big a deal. It's all just words, after all. Right?

Kind of like LBJ was just some dude . . .

I can hear my skeptics already: You're not expecting me to buy into any of this, are you? There's no way possible a bunch of boarding school brats could be that damn clueless. Not popping off with a ready definition to political science is one thing, but being completely in the dark about society matters? From a private boys boarding school? And not knowing a thing about LBJ? In *Austin*, of all places? Home to LBJ High School, The University of Texas' LBJ School of Public Affairs, his Presidential Library, and not one but two high-powered radio stations still owned by the man's heirs? Come on . . . Surely, you can come up with some more believable characters, don't you think?

Before we attempt to label certain people, one way or another, maybe we need to pick apart some general assumptions. The first being that we are not talking about some Yankee Doodle prep school like you've perhaps seen in the movies. This is Texas. The movie *Dead Poet's Society* came out right about then, too, and though we might've enjoyed seeing Robin Williams in a serious and literary role or we identified with some of its characters, none of my friends were attending our school to get a jump on Harvard or Yale. Nor were they there to become future doctors, lawyers, or senators. If we finished high school, we'd done damn good. Let's just say *boarding school* was more something we could call the place, in polite company, and still get laid afterward.

In truth, *boys ranch* would be a more apt term; *residential treatment center*, the precise one. Half the guys at my facility came by court order. It was their last chance to shape up before they got sent to TYC, short for Texas Youth Commission, what the state called its juvenile *erections*—sorry, old habits and whatnot—its juvenile *corrections* program. Essentially, it's the state prison system for kids, before they become old enough, at sixteen, to move into the adult prison barracks.

I suppose legitimate concerns might now be voiced relating to my integrity or honesty in this case. Yes, we were intentional in our deceitfulness. We tried to make it sound much better than it really was because most of us were ashamed at calling the place our residence for however long we did. By and large, we were extremely different kids, but we never wanted to be. We just didn't fit in anyplace. Often, because some adult

71

we trusted did some fucked up shit to us that made us question basic societal norms at far too young an age.

Me, personally, I had some old man take after me with a hunting knife, try and turn me from a little boy to a little girl one day. A couple others who liked beating my ass pretty regular. That was the worst, really. Unless you count the fact I got passed around like cheap bourbon between a good half dozen or so truly twisted fucks—both men and women—for whom the sight of a toddler must have been something akin to flipping the pages of *Penthouse*. So, I took to running away and hiding out in the brush as a defense mechanism. Nearly froze out there a few times, but I never got cut up like that again, either. And then one day, my mother and I went on a horribly long bus ride and wound up seeing my aunt and uncle on the coast. Not sure what all went down exactly—my mother wound up dying somehow; she was only twenty-seven—but I wound up staying there on the coast with them. They wound up adopting me, and I grew up with them, my real mother's brother and his wife, the folks I now know as Mom and Dad.

Never could anyone have guessed how ingrained and powerful that defense mechanism of mine might have been at the time. For while my life changed for the drastically better, nearly overnight, I never felt like I fit in. Not really.

All the guys I knew there were like that. We knew we were *different* from most everyone we knew, except each other. And not measuring up can play havoc with one's formative years. In fact, it sticks with you. Just becomes part of who you are. Some of us learn to channel it into something else. Others die in some gutter with needles hanging out of their arms. And still others wind up finding their own little boy and big fucking knife.

If what I've shared thus far is simply too deceitful for your tastes—you know, about our *school* being anything but—I only ask that you stick around a few moments more. All I can say is that we learned that particular trait from some of the very best while you consider the following: Texas lawmakers in 2011 voted to change TYC's name to the Texas Juvenile Justice Department (TJJD). They had the official line for doing so—something about Sunset Laws or some such—of course, none of that addressed the big goddam elephant in the room, like reports indicating child sexual abuse at TYC was so rampant that we boys who snarked about the place being the *juvenile erections program* probably had it right all along.

The findings sparked investigations, dismissals, and even a few prosecutions. They rewrote hiring practices, operational procedures, and accountability systems (they *rewrote* them, mind you, because all of these existed before), and then they sought new manpower to replace those lost in the dust up. Problem was, nobody wanted to work there anymore. Not with the scandals that took place. Became an issue of guilt by association.

So, lawmakers came up with a solution. They changed its name. That way, the very same folks who worked at very same corrupt, disgusting, child-molesting institution that TYC always had been, could then, in polite company, now say they worked for TJJD and still get laid afterward. No harm, no foul, right?

Yet I get dubbed the dishonest one . . .

So, that Johnson had been president before didn't mean jack to us. Far as we knew, there was only one, big *p* President. His name was Reagan. And unless you knew him, or were him, you didn't mess around at the White House. Keep in mind, he's the only person we'd seen live there since we started paying attention the nightly news programs our parents watched religiously. A few of us vaguely remembered someone named Jimmy Carter, but that meant even less to us than LBJ, the names Jimmy and Carter common enough to be most anyone's. Paired together, though, they just sounded right for some reason, as though we woke up one day with the name on our lips, some lingering after-effect of a dream that we couldn't remember much else about. The new dude—shrub or bush or whatever the hell his name was—only got his job because he worked for Reagan somehow. He could've mowed Reagan's yard, for all we knew. Reagan was still the only real President in our minds.

Not even that meant all that much to us. About all we got out of it was once a year in PE, one of our lard-ass coaches made us run laps until we puked while he sat in the bleachers eating doughnuts and reading the paper. Then, after our arms and legs burned like coal from all that running, he'd stand there screaming at us while we never did enough chin-ups to his liking, that huge round belly of his hanging so far over his beltline it looked like it was gonna eat those ugly polyester shorts straight off his ass. And finally, so tired we could barely move, it was sit-up after sit-up as that same coach, pacing between us, barking insults and talking about how his ninety-year-old grandmother could outdo us all—no, that wasn't a just an attempt at humor in *Dazed and Confused*; that shit really happened—all while giving us a big hairy eyeball full of his nutsack by the time class ended, those shorts never long enough to cover them bad boys up. All so we could get some bullshit physical fitness award supposedly signed the President himself. As best we could tell, Reagan was some kinda asshole who hated kids.

That, however, summed up our full and comprehensive knowledge of politics and presidents.

Now the Paramount was a real eye-opener for a skinny little twerp like me. I'd never been any place like it. Our teacher tried to prepare us, but it was sort of like explaining astrophysics to a house cat. In short, we wouldn't truly know until we'd been there and seen it with our own eyes. As to dressing nice, I had to borrow a pair a pants from a buddy of mine because mine were stylishly slashed to shreds. I wore my only button-down shirt, but even with my best high-top sneakers and my mullet, freshly trimmed and combed for a change, I still looked more like Marty McFly or Ferris Bueller than anyone destined for a night at the theatre. I was embarrassingly underdressed for the event. We all were. So much so, we loitered outside until show time and took our seats as the lights began to dim.

Over the next two hours, something magical happened. Just one guy came out on a stage with almost no set and not one prop worth remembering, yet we sat mesmerized as we all learned about someone utterly fascinating. None of us saw Sybok that night. We saw a President, a man called to power by the death of a beloved leader and friend, who even as he reluctantly took his oath of office, many were already accusing of leading an assassin's conspiracy to kill Kennedy. He inherited a war he couldn't win, a nation in chaos and enough social problems to end most people. Still, he had a penchant for snappy one-liners—my favorite to this day still: "That boy's so stupid he couldn't pour piss out of a boot if the directions were written on the heel"—and a damn-it-to-hell attitude that never heard the word no, something we couldn't help but admire.

We laughed. We cried. We ovationed.

Hell, I wanted to be this dude when I grew up—best I ever managed was attending the same university—but when the show ended, I hadn't had enough yet.

I grabbed my buddy, said, "Hey, wanna see if we can get backstage?"

He shrugged. "Why not?"

Neither of us had ever done anything like it before, but we'd been impressed. Why simply just go home? So, we hung back as the rows cleared, then made our way to the front. I'm sure we probably asked the guy they hired to pick up our drink cups, but we did it as politely as we could.

"Excuse me sir, but how do we get backstage?" I asked

him, with a level of confidence I didn't even know I had—one that simply said we may look like punk kids, but we're supposed meet the actor after the show.

The ol' boy simply pointed the way, and we were off, before he got a good look at us, to hallways unknown. It was a maze back there and mostly dark by then. We wandered about until we heard voices and then just walked toward them. By then, Turner and everyone else who came to the play with us that night had caught up to us. About the time he was going to ask us what the hell we thought we were doing, we rounded the corner and there he was: Mr. Luckinbill as LBJ. In the flesh.

He grasped our hands warmly as we made our introductions and told him we liked his show. Sadly, I had never once contemplated what I might say to the man once we got there. "We thought you were really cool as Spock's brother," seemed somehow inappropriate, and "man, for a dude we knew nothing about, you sure portrayed him well," a bit less than sincere. Thank God others began showing up right about then. And considering who they were, my crisis of commentary swiftly became irrelevant.

"Quite the performance, Mr. President," a plump, well-dressed man said, "you took me back to my oval office days, really took me back. Felt like I was right there again . . ." My head spinning still, simply from the act of getting there, I was shocked when the tubby fellow juts his pale, plump fingers at me. "Congressman Jake Pickle," he says, grasping my hand. "I was in Lyndon's cabinet. And you are?"

Realizing I'm nobody special, he returns to the actor in no time. Practiced politicians can sniff folks like me out in an instant and wouldn't bother pissing on us if we were on fire. There's simply nothing to gained, knowing someone like me, and that's all politics is, at its essence, an elaborate dance orchestrated around one core question. What can I get out of this?

"I didn't mean to be running late for your opening, so

please, a thousand apologies, but we had a big day on the Hill today, and you know, the life of a public servant," Pickle said. Honestly, I don't think a single soul realized he wasn't there until he said so. Another trait I've come to know about career politicians. They get grandiose notions about their importance in the world, like ol' Luckinbill's show couldn't have begun without him.

"I couldn't have come in at a better time, though," he continued. "Because that's when you had that fabulous rant at the window. You sounded exactly like him, I swear, your pacing back and forth. You nailed it. It looked just like it did when we had the Oval office—Lyndon, in front of those windows, the light. Everything. The way I got in, you see, every day I worked there, I'd walk in through the secretaries' pool, right past Mrs. Kopenski's desk, I believe it was—lovely creature, she was—but if you took that entrance to the Oval Office, it led to the door that would open up to that very scene, precisely. It was the same angle, same curtains, everything. I tell you, I could practically smell Mrs. Kopenski's perfume, that's how good a job you done."

Luckinbill raised a hand and with is other patted his own chest. "Thank you so much," he said. "You flatter me. I simply studied archive footage of the man himself. But you actually knew the man, saw those times from the Oval Office looking out. The stories *you* must have . . ."

"Well that rant I mentioned—Lyndon flat could not abide those protestors right there outside on the grounds like they were," Pickle said. "He took every word said like it was a personal attack against him. He never could separate the office from the man. Those hippies got to him especially, and every day brought busload after busload more to town. Something a lot of people may not realize is that 1969 'the Summer of Love' was one of the hottest summers on record at the capitol. So we would look out from the White House and see nothing but hair and signs and stink and—yeah, I believe that's the day it began—we were getting briefed on the situation in Vietnam, and Lyndon asked how many boys we'd lost. The number was awful, and it clearly upset him, so he sort of wandered away, like he would do at times like that, and stood by the window. Back at the table we moved on about some technical matter dealing with logistics. Lyndon's over there, quiet, and I take that was the first time he'd heard because he came completely unglued—that chant, the one that drove him crazy to hear—"Hey, Hey, LBJ, How many babies did you kill today?"

"Those God damn rhymes they kept calling," Luckinbill said, stepping back into character. "All night long, they just kept at it and kept at it. Why poor Ladybird couldn't get a wink of sleep. Just everywhere, far as you could see, them damn hippies, just stink and hair and signs, like a bunch of damn crazy people."

"Exactly!" Pickle shouted, quite nearly beside himself.

"It always tickled me whenever he used my name at one of the press briefings," came a maternal voice from behind us. "I made the mistake of telling him as much once when we were out on one of his early campaign trips, and he tried work me in every time he could from that point forward. Sad part was, those kids out on the lawn didn't bother me a bit. Lyndon fussing about them like he did is what kept me awake."

"Missus Johnson, how lovely of you to stop by," Luckinbill said, arms outstretched as if she might come bounding into his arms like one of those slow-motion meadow scenes between star-struck loves.

"It was one of the first speeches I ever heard him give, back when he had to borrow the money from my father to afford him a suit so he could go Austin," she said. "I could always tell when he thought he was dealing with something truly important, though, because that's when he would work my name into it somehow. His way of letting me know, even at some the most difficult times our nation faced during his service, that he was thinking of me, I guess."

The First Lady continued with her same dignified grace toward him, grasping his hand with both of hers as Luckinbill leaned in for a peck on her cheek. "So very good to see you again, Lawrence," she told him, eyes twinkling. "Marvelous performance out there today. You should be well pleased."

"Thank you so much," he said, uncertain if he should embrace her or curtsey or what. Instead, he grasped her two hands with his. "You don't know what that means, coming from you."

"And Jake," she said, "It's been a while. How have you been?"

"So much better seeing you here now," he said, hugging her warmly. "I was telling Mr. Luckinbill here how much his performance brought back the old days for me."

"Indeed," she said, returning her gaze to the actor and making eye contact with him before she turned to us. "And who do we have here?"

Thank goodness Turner reacted when did because our feet were frozen to the floor, petrified. "Mike Turner," he said, also grasping her hands with both of his. "We met at the McCombs School of Business commencement last spring."

"I remember," she said, smiling warmly. "It's good to see you."

Turner, realizing, I think, that we'd all suddenly gone statue, made our introductions for us. She greeted us all warmly in turns, then spent time with each of us, individually, regal and confident, yet equally magnanimous as she genuinely listened to what each of us had to say. Meanwhile, the congressman and actor talked quietly about the show and his craft, but one fact was certain: We may have come to ogle over an actor who had put on a show that impressed us, but Lady Bird, once she arrived, was hands down the most important person there that night.

Even ol' Jake Pickle yielded the floor to her and didn't seem the least bit put off by doing so. She was the closest I'd ever been to something even close to actual royalty, and she embodied it in every aspect, wholly. Having visited with us all, she stepped back, permitting us to reform as a single group once more, as she addressed the actor once again.

"You know, I got a call earlier this week when the *Statesman* saw that you would be opening your show here tonight," she said. "I gave them a few quotes for the story they ran, but I can't tell you how surprising it is that no one from the press was here tonight to cover all this."

What possessed me to say it when I did, I'll never know. All night long I stood there, speaking only when spoken to, dazzled by those I was surrounded by. Let's just say that if you told me I'd be standing around backstage at the Paramount with a Grammy Award-winning actor, a long-serving Congressman and a former First Lady, reminiscing a presidency that three hours prior I couldn't have told you a thing about, I would've told you to sober the fuck up because you obviously had me confused with someone else. It's a momentary flash that recurred every so often throughout my years of chasing news stories, especially after meeting someone especially popular or powerful, that how-in-the-hell-did-I-wind-up-here moment, little ol' me from nowhere, talking to the type of people that most folks only ever see on television, or over the heads of about a nine million other people as said celebrity scoots off to whatever celebrity event happens to be on his celebrity calendar that day, leaving Mr. Average and Ordinary to question their own eyeballs. *Was that so-and-so? Couldn't be. What would he be doing here? It was just someone who looked like him. Couldn't have been him for real because they've got entire agencies and departments designed to keep people like me away from people like him. Don't they?*

Right then, that timid little turd was nowhere to be found.

"I'm going to be a reporter one day," I announced, with not the least bit of uncertainty.

"And you'll be a magnificent one," Lady Bird said, patting my cheek, not long before she bid her farewells and we all parted ways.

I felt about forty feet tall leaving there.

Thank God she said what she did, when she did, too, because that was exactly what I needed to hear at that moment. Not only that, but it could've gone south any number of ways. Just imagine if my voice had cracked, mid-sentence, saying it. That would've stolen some of the wind from its sail, right from the get-go. Seeing it now in black-and-white, just sort of hanging there, unrequited—an unre-quested interjection that truly followed no logical progression whatsoever—had Ladybird chosen to simply ignore it and just left me hanging, I'm pretty sure I might have melted into cracks on the floor. I'd've left there feeling a lot closer to two inches tall, that much was certain. Plus, knowing that group of guys I was with, I'm also pretty sure that forever thereafter, I would have been my own punchline. "I'm gonna be a reporter one day," that thing you'd say in your dorkiest voice whenever someone tossed out something completely off-the-wall and got left standing there, hung out to dry, to look like a world-class dumbass.

And who wouldn't prefer forty to two? In fact, I still point to that day as a deciding moment whenever someone asks me why I chose this writer's life. Course, Turner leaning over to me as we pulled away, saying, "You really ought to write this down," didn't help matters much, either.

By the time we back to the ranch, me and a few of the others—all passengers in the same van that night—hatched this hairball scheme to launch a school newspaper. We even had a catchy title, we all thought. *The Westwood Writeup*. It was a hellova better than some of the alternatives, like *The Political Science Club Monitor* or *The Boys Ranch Roundup*, that last one sounding more like a police action than something you read for fun. I stayed up all night, writing away, with pen and paper. Our first edition, published a few days later by means of one of the office secretary typists and a photocopier, featured tons of bad puns, a community poll on some topic of great import (like what's your favorite shoe brand?), a couple hand-drawn political cartoons based on actual news headlines at the time—I remember one of them featuring a boat captain who looked an awful lot like Sean Connery in *The Hunt for Red October* had fucked Yosemite Sam and had this horrid-looking, wire-haired brat, complete with one of those old school lollipops, big as your head, who was claiming the keys from dear ol' dad, holding a half spent liquor bottle in one hand and a ginormous janitor keyring in the other, one huge skeleton key on it, beneath a caption that read "Sure son, you can drive my oil tanker just this once"— my political statement on the Exxon-Valdez oil spill, which made all the headlines back then—and a two-page writeup about our first club outing, our plans for the next one, complete with a rather snarky third-person retelling (yeah, third, I can't explain it either; sort of gonzo, but with somebody else) of our post-play backstage adventure, written and headed by yours truly. Wound up being the most awful piece of journalistic prestige you ever laid eyes on, and my peers voted me its editor-in-chief. I kept that awful rag limping along almost a year before I wound up leaving the place myself. Far as I know, the paper was gone just soon as I was.

And you know what else? Me and all those nerds who found themselves in this story to start with because we sat around playing D&D together. We went from being wedgie and wet willy targets to the newspaper guys, those same jocks and rednecks who used to whup our asses on the regular, were now sidling up to us, wondering how they, too, might contribute a story, or, as remained a constant question whenever I visited with the general public as a member of the working press, *When are y'all gonna cover* _____? Fill that blank with whatever you please because, I'm pretty sure, I already heard it, at some point or another.

Still, our title did have a snappy ring to it, I always thought.

A bit like *The Pflugerville Pflagg* or *The Jefferson Jimplecute*, but different.

Way different . . .

Regardless, meeting Lady Bird and Luckinbill like I did was a thrill like no other, something I knew I'd need repeat again, the sooner, the better. I did, too. Met singers and songwriters, authors and actors, actresses and athletes. Got to know every governor my state has had since Ann Richards was at the helm, along with nearly every other state office holder in Texas, too. I met every President our country has had from Jimmy Carter to Dubya, even shook hands with former English Prime Minister Tony Blair and President Nicolas Sarkozy from France.

For all the famous folks I've come to know through the years now, none were nearly as thrilling for me as the ones from *that* day, all those years back, there at the Paramount. Some came close, but none will ever top the original with Lady Bird and Luckinbill. Hard to improve that one. After all, I'd never known anything like it before. It was my first time.

So, blame Lady Bird, if you're reading this, wondering, "What the hell?" Or maybe Mike Turner, that teacher, who, though perhaps fictionalized somewhat here, did indeed urge me on, saying, "You really ought to write this stuff down."

Write, I did. For twenty-five years, I wrote. More than that now, I guess, because this book didn't just write itself. Still, for all its horrid production quality, bad puns and even worse grammar and spelling, that first edition's feature on a story about that rare backstage moment with the real actors in the LBJ story was all it took. I was forever thereafter hooked. The thrill of the chase. Going all the places someone like me shouldn't be allowed, and meeting scores of people who shouldn't give me the time of day. Not to mention the actual craft of writing, of holding the pen as it presses into paper.

Or watching stories unfold with characters I created, some based on real life folks, others merely pigments of my imagining. And feeling that burn of a deadline bearing down. I love it. I loved it all.

Pulitzer Prize winner and former *Washington Post* reporter Annie Hull put it like this: "It becomes your life. You give up everything to follow the story, and it's worth it. Your feel fully alive when you're reporting. It's an addiction, and once you've done it, how could you not want to be a reporter?" Almost everyone I knew in the profession felt that way. Most of us readily agreed we'd do it for free if we had to, just for the rush. What we didn't realize, not so very long ago, was that we might have to one day. A lot sooner than anyone anticipated, too. Just as I'd found my groove, it seemed, it all came crashing down.

I read Hull's words not long ago in a book called *The Morning Miracle* by Dave Kindred, a former newspaper reporter and editor, about the year *The Washington Post*, one of the most prestigious papers on the planet, did something few had ever done before—won six Pulitzers in a single year—the exact same year that it also had to downsize its staff, by about half, just to keep the lights on. Bureau offices the world over closed. Hundreds lost their jobs, including Hull, one of the Pulitzer winners.[16]

A downsizing like that you never really recover from. To be honest, it's not really *The Post* anymore. Not really. Sure, something gets printed still that calls itself *The Post*, but it's not *THE POST*, not like before.

None of them are.

Institutions of the news world, both large and small, aren't anything close to what they once were. I knew things had gotten rough in the business, but I had no idea *how*

16 Dave Kindred, Morning Miracle Inside The Washington Post: A Great Newspaper Fights for Its Life, (New York: Doubleday, 2010).

rough or how *widespread* the industry's failings truly reached. Not until I got over my own bitterness about what happened to me and began to read some about it. Not that I'm fully recovered, mind you. I still fight the urge to hock a loogy whenever I see those headlines glaring back at me in a checkout lane, considering how we parted ways. It's a terrible tango of love and hatred, most days. I went from having multiple subscriptions from all over the globe and reading most of them daily, to today, where I can't even tell you the last time I picked up an actual newsprint paper and read a whole story.

Six years, maybe? Seven? I don't honestly know.

Yet I've pondered extreme pay cuts, just to get back in. I may yet, if anything's still left of those grand institutions of my youth we knew as newspapers. But let's face it, none of us got into it expecting we'd become bajillionaires. My first year in the news business, I made more money bending wire to make the stands those papers sat in than I did filling the pages of the things they held. Nearly twice as much more.

But that's not what truly hurt.

Nearly a decade ago now, when I'd climbed to the top of the proverbial shit heap, having claimed most every accolade I could get for the type of writing I did, a fact that earned me top dollar for the words I wrote, I left that job in June to finish out the rest of the year as a walk-on hand at a construction site. It was then, wondering how my old, out-of-shape ass would still have enough *umph* left to keep up with the far younger, far more acclimated workers than I, as we all braved a searing summer to complete a multi-story county courthouse, that I wound up earning more money, running power tools all day, than I ever made clicking these little keys.

Sad to think that a job that demands I hold at least one college degree before they'll even let me in the door—honestly, at my experience level, they'd prefer I hold multiple degrees—pays less, way less in most cases, than a job most anyone can do. You and your coworkers don't even need to know the same language.

That's a sad, bitter truth.

The reporter may hold decades of experience, or hundreds of thousands of dollars in student loan debt, just getting what he needs to begin said job. He may have won more awards than he can keep track of, earned by consistent excellence in said field. Yet a fellow who arrives in the country the day before can hop off a truck and, using a borrowed tool in a country he shouldn't even be in, easily earn four or five times what that reporter can even dream about.

That's why we need that wall, some may argue.

Maybe so. But the fellow I'm describing was here already, almost a decade ago now. That wall ain't gonna keep him out. And while I'm sure those in charge will no doubt see that no illegal foreign nationals are allowed on the actual jobsite, once the wall finally does go up, how much do you want to bet that the sites the where all the *legal* workers get pulled from—all those projects that will otherwise go on hold while the builders who get tapped for the wall finish up there—suddenly don't get far more lax in their hiring practices for replacement workers to keep those other projects progressing on schedule? Let's face it, we only have a limited number of construction workers to go around. You start talking projects that enclose an entire national border, those builders will have come from someplace. For or against a wall in principle, I doubt the rich and powerful are willing to wait until it's built before their resort becomes operational, or their manufacturing plant or retail center can hire a single employee.

Have to wonder, too, if that real, *big-p* President from my youth, the one who famously said "Tear down that wall!" in reference to a similar structure built across the heart of Berlin, had spun around in his grave as our modern leadership touted a building project that history proved, thousands of years ago in China, is less than foolproof when it comes to successfully isolating yourself from the rest of the world. That assumes our man in question ever cracked a history book—or any book, for that matter—and why these words are probably safe from ever being found out.

I didn't Tweet them at two-thirty in the morning.

Although news and I may have had our issues, I can't begin to tell you how much it chaps my ass to hear the regular slams lobbed daily at the news industry, even on pander-puff outlets like *Fox News*, the heartbeat of all things conservative in our country, who proudly (and ironically, considering the latter half of their own name) report on elected leaders who claim every story they don't like is somehow the result of "fake news."

That same cheap ploy has been used by cheats, cons and liars ever since . . . well . . . ever since newspapers arose—right here in our very own country—before we could even call ourselves a country. Newspapers formed to expose the slimy, sleazy bastard pricks—those we might hand all our power in the world, faithfully trusting they might behave otherwise—whenever they, in fact, turn out to be every inch the lying, cheating, slimy, sleazy bastard pricks we all feared they could be.

Not surprising, I don't think, that the slimiest, sleaziest, lyingest cheats of them all should come to power just as the news industry limps along at its weakest. Speaks volumes to the consistency of his spine, too chickenshit to pick such a battle back when ink flowed as freely as dollars now seem to in and out of his bank accounts.

I may be plenty of things myself—believe me, I know—not least of which is some fuck up from a boy's ranch.

But how sad will it be for those generations hence, ones who never knew the likes of a good newspaper? Simply because some lying cheat tainted enough views to kill what few revenue streams they once earned.

I'm proud to say I remember the glory days of the newspaper. I regularly read good papers. Several of them, in fact. Though it's sad to have to clarify that I used the past tense of the verb *read* in this instance.

At least I got to contribute. I did once, anyway. Perhaps that's all any of us really get to say.

BUMBOOZLED

I sneak through the door, forty-seven minutes late for my afternoon shift, hoping nobody notices. It doesn't work. Before the door shuts behind me, my editor is staring me down, motioning me to his desk.

I'm in it for a right shitty day, I can tell already.

Of course, you never would've known it by the look of me. Not back then anyway. Had to prove I was worthy of the prize I thought my being in that place was. I had a helluva lot more Labrador in me than junkyard dog, back then. Don't worry, I'll grow a few fangs soon enough. You'll have to forgive me—the elder me, that is—if I should wander in from the shadows just long enough to scream *"Dumbass!"* and disappear again. Watching the kid in action gets tiring sometimes. But you'd swear his editor just wagged a box of bowser biscuits under his nose, the way he pranced over there, too damn eager to please.

Just know—he, or me—we, as it were, get better with age.

Part of it, I think, came from the fact that I was smooth terrified of my editor back then. Of course, everything I feared, back then, I'd learn to admire, twenty years down the road. We'd probably be great friends if you tacked twenty years on. Until then, he was more like a stern father figure, enforcing all the rules, because people like me insisted on breaking them.

Turns out, though, that father-figure editor, the one with

the booming voice, was the one responsible for bringing the boy me out to this desolate, dry, faraway place. Despite more than a few misgivings from others in the room. The kid had never batted in the big leagues before, the new city desk chief told the skeptics—editors, all of them, the shot callers, as it were, when it came to what, and in this case, *who*, got to grace their hallowed newspaper pages—but the kid still deserved his chance, he told them. Having worked at the daily that covered the small town where the kid lived and worked last, he told them, do you have any idea how many times, there, that kid—by himself and publishing just twice a week—scooped his entire freakin' daily staff whenever they wound up covering the exact same event? The rest eventually granted their consent, but the boy was *his* problem, they made clear. They remained skeptical—dubious at best—fully expecting him to fail. Sink, they told his editor, or do swimmingly, it would rest upon the editor's rather sizable shoulders. Such talks always happened, of course, behind closed doors. The boy, never the wiser, doubted the whole time anyone even knew he was there.

"Whatcha working on?" the editor's voice booms. He never says much. Just three words—maybe five, depending on how you write it down—but hints of annoyance hang on his breath.

"Whatcha got?" I say, arms spread wide as I pop my best *cholo* chin jut.

He's not impressed.

Behind him, fellow reporters' heads are randomly popping up from behind the periwinkle-carpeted partition walls of their cubicles. Nosey sons-of-bitches! Always gleefully awaiting the next victim. Their doing so, however, only confirms the annoyance I thought I'd detected.

"Corporate sent down word today," he said, "we need to take a more proactive approach in covering this whole Railroad Killer thing . . ."

I nod, trying to look thoughtful and engaged. Truth is, I look more like a bobble head than anything close to engaged. *"Dumbass!"*

Still, I use that brief lull in conversation to kickstart my brain. I recall some headlines from about three months back out of the Houston area on some mysterious lurker, raping and killing little old ladies, asleep in their houses, and then disappearing into the night. Investigators seemed certain the murderer hopped freight trains to make his escape. It had grandma losing her mind at Thanksgiving that year. Mind you, she lived no place near a train but claimed one of the victims had been a cousin or some such. Grandma came smooth unglued when Aunt Betty tried to open a window that day. Like the killer, perched just outside, was waiting for someone to unlatch a window so he could crawl inside, rather than use the door, three feet to the left, standing open and wide. The killer would then rape us all—all nineteen of us, one after the other—right there on the table next to the turkey and cranberry sauce. Nobody was safe. Not even that teacup Chihuahua my cousin's wife kept in her purse. When he'd had his fill, finally, he'd kill us all dead, dead, dead!

This fellow must've had the stamina of three hundred plow horses, was all I could figure.

But surely that couldn't be the same guy my editor was talking about. Thanksgiving was months ago and at least ten hours from our second-floor newsroom.

"He got moved to the *FBI's Top 10 Most Wanted List* today," the editor says. "The cops desk is working on a local angle for that, and the business desk is on the horn with Union Pacific to see what added security measures they might have in place . . ."

He pauses. I'm back being a bobble-head again— *"Dumbass"*—and though I may not *look* it, I'm actively think-ing, if the cops beat has *this* covered and the business desk on *that*, why in the world is he talking to . . .

"So the guys at corporate figure this killer could be anywhere by now. And heaven forbid we don't do our part as a *responsible* news agency to drum up a little fear every now and again. We need to make folks care about this story. So, what I want you to do is find me some homeless people—hobos, preferably—I wanna hear how *they* feel about a possible killer in their midst."

You gotta be shittin' me. That's about the stupidest fuckin' idea I've ever heard.

I didn't say that then, of course. Instead, I stood there, head still bobbing like I'm keeping beat to a Motown record..

He looks up at me. Blinks once or twice. I can't tell if he's waiting for me to say something or wondering why I'm still standing there. Behind him, it looks like the master's level of the Whack-A-Mole game for all the reporters' heads popping up from behind those partitions.

I swallow, far more audibly than I intended. "OK," I manage, "when do you want it?"

His face goes totally blank, expressionless, as eyes everywhere fix on me. Would've thought I was some medical idiot, like I'd uttered the five stupidest words fathomable in a daily newsroom. It feels like a full hour ticks by before he finally says something.

"Today, of course."

Everyone together now: *You incredible dumbass!*

I had a smiley face coffee cup, back in those days. It lived on top of my computer, its innards white with rank mold, which went well with my pigsty of a cubicle, my cheap fiberboard desk so heaped with scribbled-on notepads, pink message notes laden with indecipherable script, and reams of stray faxes and other printouts, it was a miracle every day it didn't bury me alive. I used that cup once, I think, my first day there. "What kind of newsroom *sells* coffee by the cup?" I'd asked a passing coworker, partly hoping to break the ice but mostly because I was honestly appalled by such malfeasance. Newspapers, in my experience, were printed with caffeine and ink, in that order. Dude stared at me like I just crapped on the carpet, right in front of the vending machine, then he walked off, shaking his head and mumbling something I couldn't hear.

Everyone acted like that there.

Seemed like the big-city reporter disliked *everybody*, fellow reporters most especially. The *only* conversations I ever heard there were arguments between various newsroom factions. Reporters vs. editors. Photographers vs. writers. Columnists vs. copydesk. Sports writers vs. advertising reps. Each piece of the working whole so compartmentalized and combative, it's amazing we got anything on the stands each day. It was nothing like the smaller papers I'd been used to. I simply didn't fit in there and getting hired on as a "general assignments" writer didn't help at all. It only amplified the fact that I had no place within the existing battle zones.

I trudged back to my cubicle, mulling my next move. Not every day you get told to dig a gold bar out of a goat's ass and do so without laying so much as a finger on the goat. I even pondered, momentarily, cleaning up.

Instead, I took a seat, eyes fixed on my moldy cup. Others had orderly displays of Happy Meal toys. Shelves of rare imported beers, many now decades old, hand-delivered by grateful readers from around the globe. Or massive ivy garlands entangling their now faded but still terrified assortment of Garfield cats—the kind that once adorned the rear windshield of every passing minivan, right next to a caution-yellow "baby on board" sign, proudly displayed as the driver flipped you the bird while veering on two wheels across your lane and five others in rush-hour traffic. The Garfields clung with suction-cupped feet to the foot-high glass panels atop those carpeted partition walls, like salad bar sneeze guards.

I had my moldy cup, its smiley face marred by a single bright red trickle that oozed from a lone entry wound above its right eye. The words *I don't give a fuck about your day!* were scrawled in angry font beneath the smile. I left it where it sat—mold and all—as my own general commentary. I linger a while at my keyboard, thinking I should probably log on and check messages. But that's soon abandoned, too, after I spot the annoyed glare my editor leveled in my direction, why-the-hell-are-you-still-here painted all over him. I grab my camera bag and head for the door.

Ol' Griff, my editor (I never called him that directly, mind you), was always "Sir" face-to-face. He could've had one of those posh editor offices along the back wall—most were larger than my whole house—but he refused it. He could've been in his posh office, behind some ginormous hardwood desk and closing doors, complete with credenzas and complementary throne upholstered in the finest Armenian leathers. But had he chosen to enjoy such fineries, he never would've nabbed my ass. I could've made it to my heap, turned in a couple of evergreen stories I kept in reserve for such occasions, and been back to my place at the lake, fishing in less than forty-five minutes and leaving that hobo-hunting assignment for some other poor bastard. That's how it worked *after* he moved away to that Oklahoma City paper, anyway.

That's not how ol' Griff worked, though. He latched onto one of those cheap particle board desks, just like the rest of us peons. Rather than leave it where it sat in its partition wall maze, he dragged it over near the copy desk, in plain view of the outside doors, the breakroom, and the restrooms.

Aside from catching us delinquents, his locating there offered several other perks. He didn't have to shout across the room, pick up a phone, or walk his sizable ass to tell the folks on the copy desk, who built all our pages, that pictures might be ready, or a story might need replacing. Him locating there made me ever-conscious of my progress (or lack of it) on every assignment he gave me, just in case he should ask. And I can't tell you how many walk-about time-killing trips to the Coke machine or bathroom or cigarettes outside his position there ultimately discouraged.

My hand already on the knob, he booms once more. "Good luck." It startles me, and I jump. He sits there, odd little smile, just fucking with me, I'm sure. I readjust my camera bag, toss him a half-assed wave and get the hell out of there before he does something else that'll puzzle me for hours. Back then, in my twenties, he drove me smooth nuts.

Downstairs, I sign one of the crappy Hondas out of the motor pool. Eight cars in all, each one's about as trashed as my desk upstairs and all are in varying degrees of disrepair. If we drove *them*, gas was free. If I used my own truck, it was on my tab, and after Friday nights at the bar, there was never much tab left. So, I relied on those staff cars quite a bit, but it could be a crap shoot each time you signed one out. They might smell like feet, yesterday's liverwurst, or worse. They even left you stranded, time to time, and given my current assignment, I hoped for one that didn't last three blocks. Then it would be the car, not me, that could be blamed when I had no story.

Wouldn't you know it? This one ran like new. I pull out in the street and point toward the tracks in search of anybody walking around 2 p.m. on a Wednesday. Of course, it's also about nine billion degrees in the shade, and you'd have to search far and wide to find any tree taller than a water cooler in this pitiful stretch of West Texas wasteland. That was particularly true of railyards most anyplace. You could stand at one end of town and see twenty miles in either direction without trying too hard. Unless my hobos had a hankering for asphalt grilled eggs, chances of finding one out for a stroll were next to none.

I head to the park. They've got a tree or two, and I read a

few police reports that said the homeless sometimes camped there. None are situated far from the tracks. Only thing is, they go on for miles. Just finding them is going to take a while.

My mind wanders. Why the hell did I get such a raw deal? I found the group that trained search dogs, providing our first local angle when tornados tore late night swaths through large residential sections in Oklahoma City, my first day on the job. I brought them the story about that kid, drowned at the lake, even tracked down a local color piece based on an offhand comment some of the locals made, watching divers surface with a half-filled body bag, about how the "Lady of the Lake" claimed yet another. (Although not unlike *La Llorona* tales told all across the Southwest, the local legend linked its wailing woman to murderous Cheyenne raids and a hundred-fifty-year-old gravestone, set in the long-shadowed ruins of an old frontier fort, a place so spooky even the U.S. military dubbed the place Fort Phantom). I found all sorts of feel-good pieces, too. New zoo exhibits. A new ice hockey team. Cowboy poets. Chuckwagon cookoffs. Even a first-of-its-kind Kid Town Safety Center, the brainchild of local state troopers, where kids commandeered go-carts to traverse an entire kid-sized town with real working traffic lights and surprise obstacles, all designed to teach children the rules of the road. Of course, we all lived in the real world, at the same time. A fluff piece on local inmates becoming new GED graduates, for instance, might include the same list of names when prison riots turn deadly. I'd written all those and more in the nine months I'd been there, which is why a bullshit assignment like this one made no sense at all.

But the icing on the cake, the true *coup d'é·tat,* came the day I broke the story on a local shooting, something our newspaper almost never got to do. Not with four local TV stations, two news radio stations, and three other newspapers all vying to be the first to bring folks at home the news. I can't begin to tell you the number of times a TV reporter, standing next to me on a scene, would break into their programming, whatever time of day, to say almost nothing but break the story just the same. "We're here at the corner of First and Church Streets downtown at what appears to be the scene of a crime. So far, no one has said anything about what's taking place here, but someone has indeed cordoned off the scene with what appears to be half a mile of yellow tape. We'll bring you the full story at five. Until then, this is Dude Goodhair, Channel 15 News . . ." To scoop all those bastards was a rare treat indeed, and boy, was it ever a doozy.

I flick on my blinker, turn into city park, and head for the tree line, the beginning of close to 100 miles of meandering roadways and hiking trails. I slump back in my seat. This is going to take forever.

Anyway, my story, the newspaper's last full-fledged scoop? A local cop shot and killed a man in the alley behind his house. His crime? Gardening, best I could tell, and out of season, at that. But no simple sound bite, as is usually the case, would ever get this story told. Not by a long shot, it turned out.

The humble police scanner, in the right set of hands, was once the greatest of all reporter tools, if you had even the slightest notion of what you were hearing. Of course, I preface that statement with *once*, as in way back when. The cell phone had killed the scanner in modern day. But here's what I heard: A patrol cop took a disturbance call, and seemed to wander, lost, for several city blocks, before calling for backup, real excited, and then everything went silent, for more than an hour. The next check I heard, from the exact same location, was the police chief's number, and a call went out asking for a justice of the peace.

That the chief should arrive was a bit strange, considering the man typically wore neckties more expensive than my entire wardrobe, and rarely left his office except to go home or hand out awards. What really tingled my Spidey senses, though, was that the chief, of all people, called out a JP. I was a bit surprised when a town the size of Abilene—with two major hospitals, an Air Force base, three high schools, and three universities—didn't have a medical examiner, a fact I'd learned with the drowned kid story. So, like most of the little towns I covered up until then, they would send for a JP, who ordered an autopsy, and the recently deceased got a free ride to the examiner's office in Lubbock.

But that wasn't my beat, not *then*, anyhow. I might've covered cops on weekends or during breaking events, late at night. But I was to never mistake those *stand-in* duties as anything but that. A point that was made abundantly clear to me.

I've noted before how less than genial fellow reporters often were. But I learned quick to not let it *appear* you were sniffing around another reporter's turf. Beat reporters were the absolute worst. They got rabidly possessive of anything even remotely related. Touch on anything that could've (or, in their minds, *should've*) been *their* story, and you were treading on none-too-solid ground.

To look at her, you wouldn't expect she was half raving lunatic. A Winona Ryder look-alike with Southern Belle demeanor and, when she wanted, a honey-kissed Georgia-peach drawl that made most of the old farts she worked for information simply quiver. She used a similar tact in the newsroom whenever she had something she needed to get done. But stay just one minute longer than she felt necessary, and Southern Belle would turn sidewinder in a big goddamn hurry. My first weekend working cops, I made the mistake of following up a story from the day before. After talking to a couple of sources, I learned I was the second person from the paper to ask about it. Back at the office, I got my ass reamed up one side and down the other—it's how I learned how possessive a beat reporter might be.

Another time I came in early after one of those week-end shifts to pass along some information I had on a story that hadn't finished yet when my shift came to an end. She shut me down before I got four words out. Someone of her expertise and training had no need of anything, *ever*, from a dumb hick like me. She didn't want me thinking we two might somehow be peers. She had two journalism degrees from Syracuse, by God. If she ever had a grammar question, she might pay me and my English degree a visit. She doubted it, though, especially not from some chickenshit state school like mine.

"Well, fuck you very much, bitch!" I remember saying.

That night.

When I got home.

Looking in the mirror, to see what those words might look like, coming out of my mouth. I damn near broke down crying, that afternoon, when that crazy bitch tore my ass sideways for trying to pass on some information. If that wasn't bad enough, the managing editor came and bit a chunk off my ass later (I found out she was fucking him, but only after they both left for Forth Worth when his promotion came through, even though his wife—the spitting image of Julia Roberts—spent a week in our office, packing him up for the big move).

Still, when he came to chew on me some more, I think I *did* cry a little. *"Dumbass!"* he loved asking a question, then hollering "Well . . . *Well* . . ." Then, as soon as you'd answer, he'd cut you off. This was *his* fuckin' house . . .

You get the idea. This event—the one with the domestic call, the police chief coming in for backup and needing a JP—all took place during the real reporter's watch, not mine. So, I passed on any suspicions I might've had from the scanner that day. Besides, Miss Syracuse would've had it already. When I saw nothing written, nothing on the evening news, I figured it was nothing. You should've seen the chief detective's color drain when I made a passing remark a couple of days later (on *my* appointed day). I don't recall my exact phrasing, but it was something along the lines of "heard your boss actually had to work for a change the other day."

In no time flat, I was in the chief's office with four detectives and the public affairs man. Turns out, it had been a mighty big goddamn deal, and as one of them confided to me weeks down the road, one they thought they'd managed to keep quiet.

The officer in question got called to that location to investigate a situation where a man wearing blue jeans and a plain white T-shirt was brandishing a knife at some woman who looked hurt. So, the cop pulls into the alley, as they tended to do there, in hopes of surprising the aggressor or even catching him in the act. Made perfect sense so far, I said. Thing is, in that part of town, the house numbers can get squirrely. Aside from having a general notion of what block he was on (the 1300-block of Post Street, for instance), he had no idea whatsoever what the house number might be. Not in that part of town. I was familiar with the area. A buddy of mine lived nearby. Most of the yards were two or three acres, and the neighborhood was less-than-affluent, one could say. Many families brought trailers, RVs, or little wood-frame houses from someplace else, set them between existing residences, where they took whatever number might be available to start receiving mail. On this block, what should've been just four houses was closer to thirty. It was more trailer park than neighborhood.

No matter, though, the cop spied his culprit right off. Dark, shoulder length hair, ratty jeans, plain white T-shirt. He had something in his hands, too. The officer pulled up right behind the man, hopped out and drew his gun. He hollered repeatedly that he was a policeman, that the fellow needed to lie down and place his hands behind his head. That fellow, though, smooth ignored him.

The cop issued his warning at least a couple more times. Other officers who arrived on the scene were more than happy to confirm. Several seconds pass and the fellow finally spins around and looks scared as hell. He's got something behind him, though, hidden behind his leg. It doesn't look like a knife, exactly, but it could easily be a bat or a club. The officer, at gunpoint, is screaming his orders—lay down on the ground and drop the weapon—but the guy doesn't listen. He sets his jaw, stands his ground. In fact he looks straight-up defiant. That's what they tell me anyway, so I listen to what they say. Then out of nowhere, tension already high, this woman in a red dress comes flying out of the house, screaming like a lunatic and waving a bright yellow towel over her head.

I looked up at them then, this panel of policemen, telling me this tale. The whole damn story just took a turn for the surreal. They nodded in unison, as if to confirm any doubts.

The man who up to now hasn't moved an inch, sees the woman running toward him and suddenly breaks running towards her. For all the ignored warnings issued, him acting erratic and him still holding a weapon, the policeman did precisely what he was trained to do at the academy, the public affairs man said. He was just following procedure.

That sounds so much better than he shot him—Pop! Pop! Pop!—three times, once in the shoulder and twice in the back. "It appeared the suspect was about to assault the woman again with whatever weapon (a hoe, it turned out) he had tried to keep hidden from the police." That was the official statement from the police.

Wow! I said. That woman must've been truly grateful. You gotta be some kinda ballsy to go after her with a cop standing right there, gun already drawn on you . . .

Not exactly, the PIO says, eyes shifting round the other men in the room. The cop was at the wrong house entirely. In fact, because the numbers were so screwed up there, he was almost a full city block away from where he needed to be, and on the wrong side of the street. Everybody at the call location had already taken off. The woman has walked down the block to her mother's, which was where she made the call for help. The man with the knife, jeans, and plain white T-shirt—the fellow our officer thought he'd caught—took off in his truck long before the call for help was even placed.

Then who's the—

And that's where it got really messed up: Seems the dead guy, there on the ground, had made the paper a few years back, saving these kids on the other side of town from a burning house. The man's face was plastered all over the front page. In fact, one of the photographers got nominated for a Pulitzer for the series of photos he took of the man shucking his coat, wrapping his arms, and diving through flames into the house, the reemerging moments later, a toddler gripping his neck and an infant in each arm. What made the story truly amazing was that the man who ran in to save those kids was deaf as a post. He lived nowhere nearby, just happened to be driving by, saw the fire and stopped to watch. While he's standing there, the kid's mother, who barely made it out herself, saw him and ran up screaming "My babies, *my babies!*"

He didn't hear a word she said, but apparently, he read her lips, and simply took off. The woman didn't realize he was deaf until later, trying to thank him. That's when one of the firemen, who had a deaf daughter, saw him trying to sign, so he acted as interpreter. The man got all these awards from both the police and fire departments. He was even featured on Jay Leno's show, *60 Minutes, Dateline* . . . It was huge news, back then, a front-page photo, a fancy police department soirée, featuring the very same cop and that very man, arm in arm, when he'd presented this fellow with their departmental commendation for his heroism that night.

I couldn't believe my ears.

Thing was, though, it just kept getting worse.

Seems that morning, the man's little girl accidentally left the front door to the house open when they went to wait for the bus. Not a lot, but just enough for the kitten she'd gotten a month ago from Santa—in fact, that's what she named it: *Santa Claws*—to sneak out in the dark and start playing around outside.

That same morning, another officer, responding to another call, pops on his siren and lights, and guns his engine to get someplace quick. The cat, never having seen or heard such a thing, tries to run away, but the way those trailers are set, winds up running out into the street, just trying to get away. The officer swore he never saw or heard a thing, but he apparently nailed the cat with his car, right in front of the little girl and her dad, and just kept on rolling. Now the girl's freaking out, of course, so the man brings her back in, grabs a shoebox from the house, and goes to collect what's left of the cat. His wife calms the girl down and takes her to school. And while they are away, the man buries his little girl's pet in the alley behind their house.

So, he was burying his daughter's cat when the cop arrived?

Well, yes and no, the PIO said. It was dry for almost two years straight when all this happened, so the ground was like concrete. The man wasn't able to dig very deep but he thought it would be enough to at least get the dead kitten out of sight when his daughter came home later that day. Well, there are several stray dogs that run loose all around out there. The man spent the day working in the yard, which was how he later noticed those strays fighting over something that looked awfully familiar. They dug it up, of course, and were now fighting over which one might get to eat it as a snack, all just minutes before that little girl was due back.

That man sees what's happening and takes after them dogs with this chopping hoe he had at his back fence. He gets the cat back, wraps it up in a plastic bag. Then he grabs a garden hose to soak the ground down so he can dig a deeper hole to get that cat out of sight before his daughter gets home.

As he had it all whipped and was packing the ground back down tight, now is when the officer arrived, thinking this man in his backyard wearing jeans and a plain white T-shirt was the one from the assault call he'd gotten.

Hang on—which was it? An assault call or a disturbance?

Let's see . . . It says here—

No, not the reports, what was he *told*?

How do you mean?

Those reports are written after everything is said and done. I'm not saying they're right or wrong, but what information was he given when he pulled up?

I got you. Don't know, but I'll check. Appreciate you thinking like that.

So, then what happened?

Of course, the man can't hear a damn thing the cop is saying. The cop thinks he's just ignoring him, and then here comes this woman, right about the same time, flailing her arms everywhere to get the deaf guys attention and trying to sign at him to drop the damn hoe. Mind you, he's kind of scared to, having just turned around to find a patrol car parked right behind him and a cop pointing a gun at him. He may have even recognized the officer, considering he gave him the award back then.

O God!

Yeah, well, the man sees his wife and tries to get to her, so she can explain everything. The officer, thinking he's still ignoring him, took him moving as a sign of aggression, and did what they trained him to do at the academy when you believe someone is acting aggressively.

So, you're telling me this cop drives up, scares the shit out of some deaf man, a fellow who is damn near canonized a saint around here six years ago, including by the cop who's drawing a bead on him, all while this dude's trying to bury a cat your department killed earlier that day. Then, as he sees his wife, obviously upset, tries to go to her and gets shot in the back three times?

The PIO nods through the entire question, his eyes now fixed, sullen, aimed at the top of his desk. Yeah, that's pretty much it. Be as kind as you can, will you?

Where was his little girl?

Inside, looking out the window. She saw the whole thing.

That's gonna make the whole being kind thing awful hard to do, I told him. He nodded, eyes back on his desk. He knew. I collected up reports from what happened, got a status report on the officer, his personnel file, even a few comments from the chief. I even paid the grieving widow a visit, met that sad little girl, who had to plum despise cops from that day forward, considering they killed her cat and her dad, both in the same day.

I came back and told ol' Griff—sir to his face, of course—that I had a story he wasn't going to believe. He was reading over it later, after I turned it in, double checking all my sources to make sure everything was correct.

"Who else has this?" he asked.

"Other than me and, now, you, I think we're the only ones in the whole town who know."

For the first time ever, and, if I'm not mistaken, the last, too, as far as I could recall, ol' Griff simply looked up at me and grinned.

That story wasn't all that long ago, which is why I can't figure why I'd be getting the shaft like this now. I come to the end of that section of park, I sit up taller because I have a major highway to cross. I pop my blinker and pull out into the cars. I make it across the highway without causing a wreck and turn onto the next batch of park roads on the other side of the highway.

So far, I hadn't seen shit that looked even close to a camp.

Back to cruising speed at another maze of park roads, my mind's back to wandering. What exactly am I gonna say when I find who I'm looking for? "Excuse me, sir, but might you be a hobo?" Hardly the best ice breaker I ever came up with. And what happens if I come across the killer himself? I'm hardly a badass. Hell, Grandma was afraid he'd take out the whole damn family. Now I'm out here all by myself, and I don't even have a phone.

I can see tomorrow's headlines already. *Idiot reporter found gutted near tracks.* My editor, quoted in paragraph three, "It's no major loss to our organization. He was always late, anyway."

That slow ass driving got to putting me on edge. I'd killed an hour already with nothing to show, and all *these* roads are set half a mile from the trees, at least. I park the car, grab my gear, and start walking. I dread the decision almost immediately. It's damn hot, and I haven't made it six steps from my ride. Already, my dress shirt is clinging to my back, sweat blotches are soaking through my khakis, and those black dress shoes feel like I strapped a couple of lit coals to my feet.

Man, I should've been to work on time.

Nearly an hour passes. I'm drenched. Sweat's dripping off the end of my nose, and I can't hardly see for the sting in my eyes. Worse still, I haven't seen a soul. Not one. *I'm* the only one ignorant enough to be hiking around in this heat. But I can't turn back. Going back to the office with no story is a firing offense. I must soldier on. I top a small rise and spot *something* on the edge of a brush line. It's still a few football fields away, but I can see a couple of fellows sitting in the shade, beside—what is that?—a creek?

I pick up my pace, but the closer I get, the more those two dudes seem to wander. By the time I get to where I first spotted them, there's no one there. I call out, camera dangling at my neck, notepad in hand; "Hi, I'm with the local paper. I'd like to interview you."

I listen. Even the birds fall silent. I stand there, alone, for several minutes before finally accepting defeat and starting that long trudge back to the car. *"Dumbass!"*

Looking back on all the dumbass shit I once did when it comes to reporting, it's amazing I ever managed to get anything out of anyone. My idea of an interview these days looks one helluva lot more like another bum happened to walk up and just started chatting it up. Most folks don't even realize they talked to a reporter until the story comes out. Of course, that came with practice over a couple of decades. I sure as hell wouldn't have been sporting a necktie and khakis to track down bums in the park like I did that day.

Of course, had my editor told me to slide into a chicken suit and stand on the corner every day from 10 a.m. to noon, I would've done it back then, especially if incentives were involved. You tell me to do some stupid shit like that now, and I'll help you figure out which orifices said chicken suit might fit in to see the least amount of daylight. It's not that I'm purposely obstinate. I'm just out of shits to give.

I drive back to the office, trying to come up with a plausible excuse. Hell. I might just head to the bar. The TV guys should be getting off soon. But halfway back, I have a stroke of genius—or maybe just a stroke—it's hard to tell one from the other, sometimes.

I dump off the shitty little Honda and hop into my truck, a jacked-up '78 Ford Ranger. As those dual glass-packs fire to life, I point my headlights home, where I shed my dripping dork attire and find my rattiest jeans and an old concert

T-shirt that I ripped the sleeves off years ago, and I grab by boots and a beat up old ball cap before latching onto a fishing pole, a cooler, and all my fridge beers. It takes me an hour to get back to the park. I glance in the mirror, looking nothing like that soggy son-of-a-bitch who invaded their camp earlier. Now that I know where the camp is, I park a lot closer, grab my pole and beer cooler, and head straight for the creek. I set up on the opposite bank from where I spotted them earlier.

I cast out my line and crack my first beer. It works like a charm. That line didn't catch shit, but the sound of the top coming off that beer sure did.

At the top of the rail on the opposite bank, two men appear, one a good head-and-a-half taller than the other, and so skinny you would've thought he might blow away. The tall one walks with a hunch, defeated, like he's lost the will to care. Perhaps, it's just his sad, pale gray eyes and vacant stare that give him such a dull pallor. He's dressed nice enough, with a red-checked button down, tucked and belted, sleeves meticulously removed. His jeans look a mite long for the sneakers he has on, suggesting either Salvation Army didn't carry his size or he normally wears boots. I envy him, however, for his lush head of hair, since mine was already growing sparse twenty years ago. This fellow's hair, though in need of a trim, looks like a burr haircut he quit tending one day. It's got a shaggy appearance, like a helmet made of fur, his sideburns, neck hairs, eyebrows—everything—are all precisely the same length as the hair on top of his head. Despite the hair gone native, he's got a handsome beard, especially for a dude who probably sleeps not far from here. A quick trip to the barber, get him to stand up straight, he could pass for any number of folks who were once known as greats: D.H. Lawrence, maybe, or Sigmund Frued. Ernest Hemingway, perhaps, in his elder, more genteel years.

The shorter, pudgier fellow makes up for all the dull or stodgy airs the tall one gives off by being a complete, utter slob. He looks like he might try to keep his face shaved, though right then, it hadn't seen a razor in at least a week. Beneath the stubble, old acne scars lined both of his round and tanned cheeks. Where the other fellow had a nice head of hair, this fellow looked like 70 percent of his hair just up and moved one day, leaving no forwarding address. He was mostly bald, kinda fat, and ugly as hell. Still, for my money, he seemed the type of dude I'd rather have on the trail. Why? Because he seemed, I guess, like he had a joke or two to tell.

He had a Cheshire Cat smile and, something else that caught my eye, especially coming down the trail where it looked a mite steep, for a fat man, he was nimble and balanced, fairly light on his feet. Other than that, he was a mess, from the dirt splotches on the baby blue surfer shorts that hung past his shins (he later told me he had ripped the ass out of his other pants sliding down a cliff, so he had to borrow a pair of boxers from the taller dude, which explained the fit) to his little-old-lady horn-rim readers that he kept in the same pocket as these ginormous bright pink novelty sunglasses. Even the unseemly tear at the belly button level in his Pink Floyd T-shirt had a function, which he later demonstrated to me by grabbing either side of his belly and squishing it just so—so that his belly actually looked like a mouth with big lips singing a whole catalogue of old soda shop tunes, which he voiced in a ventriloquist's pitchy squeal—all of it, just weird enough, even the most soulless bastard couldn't help but giggle. He had done alright for himself, he told me later, for his mom being a circus midget and his dad a rodeo clown. Growing up the way he did, nobody expected he'd ever be Bill Gates, and he didn't want to sound negative, but he'd about given up on his dream of getting signed by an NBA team.

Put them together, though, the two were just like carrots and peas. They were entirely opposite, but in complementary ways. They meander up slow, like they're just passing by, but you can spot the thirsty look on them from about a mile away. I ain't the only one who's fishing, it seems, and their catch, they won't need to scale.

"Any luck?" the tall one asks.

"Naw, I just got here," I say, lighting a smoke.

"You wouldn't happen to have another one of those, would you?" the shorter one asks.

"Sure, help yourself," I say, tossing over a half-pack. The creek is hardly the Mississippi. I don't have to throw far.

"Hang onto it," I say. "Got a fresh pack right here."

They both light up.

"Care for a cold one?" I offer, grabbing a tallboy from my stash.

"Don't mind if I do." Shorty says.

They must be thinking it's Christmas on their side of the creek. I underhand him a can. He cradles it like I just tossed him a sleeping baby. Not to be rude, I send over a second. The taller one isn't nearly as graceful.

"So, what brings y'all out today?"

"Oh, we're just out and about," Shorty says, eyes shifting.

"Really? I just moved here myself. Though I'd check out the waters, see if anything bites."

They smile and continue swilling my beer. I polish off mine and start digging around in the cooler.

"Anybody ready for a refill?"

Like I had to ask.

Halfway through beer two, their tongues start to loosen. They ask about the concert on my shirt. I say it was one hell of a show. They talk about the creek, how they both dragged up monster catfish in the past. I try to act hopeful.

The taller one eventually admits: "Yeah, we live right behind those trees up there. Got us a camp."

"No shit?" I say, sipping my beer. "That's gotta be pretty tough."

Both of their heads bob up and down.

I have 'em right where I want 'em.

"It ain't so bad," the tall one says. "Beats punching a damn clock, anyway."

I rather doubt either of these two ever did such a thing. We swig our beers again.

"So, how'd you wind up here?"

"We met in . . . Nevada, wasn't it?" he says, looking at Shorty. "Yeah, ol' Jesse here, he had him a fire going. It was cold as hell that day. We hit it right off then, and we been traveling around together ever since. Been about eight years now. Rode in on the rails . . ."

Jesse nods and lights a couple more of my cigarettes with a match.

"I'm Bobby, by the way. Don't think I caught your name."

"I'm Nathan," the taller one says. "Nathan Hand."

"I'm Jesse James," Shorty says.

"No shit? Well, how 'bout that? I go out to catch a fish and I wind up running into Jesse James. Y'all ain't gonna try and rob me or nothing, are ya?"

They both laugh, a lot louder than I really would have liked. I'm rather glad they're on *that* side of the creek. I pop my line a few times like I'm really serious about this whole fishing venture. It's now or never, I tell myself.

"So, how'd you wind up living out here?"

"Well," Nathan says, opening another beer, "I used to be a soldier. Vietnam. I was there for three years, planning to make a career of it. Jesse, here, he was a family man."

The other man nods.

"But things just don't always work out the way you got 'em planned."

"I hear ya, man," I say, digging in the cooler for another round. Just three left. I gotta wrap this up soon. . . .

"You know, I hear there's some killer wandering around out here on the tracks. Done jacked up a bunch of old ladies all over the state. Ever worry about running across somebody like that, living out here in the open?"

They laugh, cracking open my final beers.

"You meet all sorts out here," Nathan says. "But I'll tell you this: I'm a hell of a lot more concerned about fire ants when I lay my head down at night."

Gold! It takes everything I got not break off in my white boy shuffle right there. Plus, with the cooler now empty, I've got no reason to stay. And from the looks of things over there, they seem to feel the same way. I crank on my reel to bring in my line.

"I'm gonna run to the store, see if maybe they can't replace these," I tell them. "They got a serious defect, each and every one. They're fucking out of beer."

Jesse and Nathan are already headed back to camp. Someone else has arrived, too, and he's carrying a plastic shopping bag.

"Maybe we'll run across each other again sometime."

Nathan gives me a half-hearted wave over his shoulder. I take my cue.

I dump my gear in the bed of the truck and race back to the office. Ol' Griff's long gone already, but I did get some stares from folks on the copy desk, probably because of my attire. Still, no one says a word.

I plop down at my computer and get right to work.

The words are like honey.

By Bobby Horecka
Reporter-News Outdoor Residential Writer

It's fire ants, not brutal killers, that members of Abilene's homeless community say they fear most when they go to sleep at night.

That's according to Nathan Hand, who with his travel companion, Jesse James, came wandering by a shady creek bed Wednesday in Abilene. The railroad, their primary transit these days, just a stone's throw away. Still, in this isolated corner in one of the city's miles of parks, they've found a place they call home. For now, anyway. They go to sleep most nights with the stars overhead. From down there, from their view, you wouldn't believe it's just a few blocks from downtown. . .

I bang away at my keyboard, fifteen column-inches on the events of my afternoon. I tell about the men I'd just met, adding purpose to the tale with old details about the Railroad Killer himself, and details of his crimes. I couldn't have been prouder, as I gave it one last read before turning it in. Mostly because I got handed a bullshit assignment, and I still got it in.

Take *that*, you bastards!

But no one takes anything, not that day, anyway.

While I was out boozing it up with a couple bums in the park, Angel Maturino Resendiz, AKA the Railroad Killer himself, got arrested by a Texas Ranger someplace on the border near El Paso. with news of his capture saturating the news wires, no one in his right mind could give two shits about how safe a couple hobos might feel in Abilene, nearly five hundred miles from where the killer was found.

So unbeknownst to me, while I was away, the whole thing was just scrapped, and everybody goes on to live and fight another day. Can't tell you how happy I was nobody even bothered to find me, let me know that it was called off. At least I didn't wind up my own gory headline, I guess, for whatever that's worth.

Still, it kinda sucked overall. Just one thing was true:

Man, I shoulda been to work on time. But whatcha gonna do?

MR. MAN CANDY

I always take him with a few grains of salt. Not too much. I mean, dude's always been on the rotund side, and he's got a heart condition, for Christ's sake. But don't take everything he tells you at face value. You just can't. Don't get me wrong: I love Bubba to death. Known him for almost ten years now. Together, we've caught rivers of fish, travelled the world, and even started our own construction business. He's the type of dude you don't mind loaning money, the sort of fellow you toss your housekeys and ask to feed your dog while you're away, and he's absolutely somebody you want at your back in a barfight. Still, when he called me one day and said he spent the afternoon on his front porch with a Playboy Bunny, I said the first thing that came to mind.

"Bullshit," with the proper three syllables that such a statement truly deserves.

Course, he starts swearing on his mama's grave and Holy Jesus he's telling the truth. But come on! Dude lives in a one-stoplight town in the ass-crack of South Texas. Although the population sign says three thousand four hundred thirty-five, I'm pretty sure three quarters of them are inmates at the prison, the town's only employer. And my left butt cheek has more resemblance to Hugh Heffner's mansion than his ratty old trailer.

Even the word *porch* needs a few shakes of salt, to hell with his damn heart.

Step is a more accurate description.

I'll be damned if the ol' boy didn't prove me wrong. Again . . .

Before you start calling me a straight-up asshole, you've got to understand how we two met. Bubba and me, that is. I ain't losing any sleep over what you may call me. I've been called worse. A lot worse. Today, even, and the sun ain't even up good yet. Still, how we met says an awful lot to how we've put up with each other so long. It says a lot about what makes us tick, how we view the big wide world around us.

Hard to believe, but there was a time—not terribly long ago—that Bubba and me hadn't said word one to each other yet, despite having been on the same jobsite for going on six months. I'd seen him around, but that was it. Simply put: We worked different crews in different trades. He's a framer, which is a lot like a carpenter for any of y'all never worked on a building crew before. Big difference is that most carpenters work exclusively with wood—cabinets, finish trim, that sort of thing—a framer may do a little woodwork, but mostly, he deals in steel and drywall, the preferred mediums of modern commercial construction. Me: I'm an electrician. We follow along right behind the framers to put in everything electrical. We've got the drywall guys behind us, the tape-and-float guys behind them, so on and so forth, through every trade—pipefitters, plumbers, HVAC, concrete, floor finishers, roofers, windows—it's one big assembly line, one trade after another, until we're done.

We finish ahead of schedule, there's bonuses; works with penalties, if we're behind because it ain't just your part held up. The crews behind you are legion, and they're all juggling schedules and jobsites, trying to keep their guys working every day and the whole project moving forward. Nowadays, too, there's no telling how many different crews you may get at a single site or what language they all speak, so they talk dollars.

Everybody understands dollars.

Call it an unwritten rule, construction or otherwise, but most learn it pretty quick. Don't fuck with other crews and they won't fuck with you back. Makes everything a hellova lot easier, most days. And if I learned anything in the years I put in, it's this, I work around all sorts of people in a day's time, the kind of work I do. You might be dealing with honest-to-God, real-life geniuses one minute and talking at people who don't even know the words coming out of your mouth the next. So, you never assume a damn thing on a jobsite. You assume something, kind of work I do, somebody winds up *dead*. Electricity don't give a shit. Jump to hasty conclusions without double and triple checking simple facts first, it'll smooth cook you from the inside out. It don't even give a damn who else it takes out in the process.

Long story short, were it not for landing on the same floor that afternoon—and that dumbass kid—I doubt we ever would've said word one to each other, ol' Bubba and me.

Every crew has its dumbass. That kid was theirs.

I'd seen hands like him a thousand times: This fresh-out-of-the-box, know-it-all little prick who couldn't keep his yap shut if you paid him. He knew every obscure fact about how the Martians built the pyramids and how his piss-ant wages were single-handedly funding the welfare system—I know this because he told us, *all morning long*—but somehow in all his expertise, he hadn't yet mastered the fine art of working a tape measure.

Not by a little, either, like he hadn't got them fractions quite yet. *No.* Every stud he touched ran shy by at least an inch—up to and *including* five—*inches*, that is, *shy* of the wall he was building. Gets downright irritating. Make you wanna lose your mind. Believe me. I've seen plenty who did.

But not Bubba. No sir.

He drew that kid in close, tucked him right under those big ol' dragon wings of his.

"Gaaw-lee," I heard Bubba say, right after lunch. "This one's coming up short, too."

He sounded as perplexed as that kid must've been, standing there, squinting up at him and biting his lip. There wasn't an ounce of meanness in it, nothing Bubba said, just a kindly observation offered in the sweetest granddad baritone.

Ol' Bubba played it, too. He doffed his hat, scratched his big shaggy head. Would've thought he was working out astrophysics the way he was thinking it all out. He even busted out a pencil, started working it out in longhand in the rafters, way up there.

"Boss is gonna be awful mad, we keep going through studs like this," Bubba says in that same sticky sweet drawl. Even clear across the building, you could see those words take all the wind out of that kid. His shoulders slumped. Feet shifted. Almost felt sorry for the little bastard.

Bubba had him right where he wanted. He puts on his best thinking face, stroking his beard for a couple minutes as if it dripped answers, then suddenly lights up.

"Yeah," he says, but almost immediately shakes his head and rules out whatever it was.

"That wouldn't possibly work. Unless . . ."

He's full-on working out imaginary long division problems now, right down to carrying the one with his pinky finger. His cyphering seems to've uncovered some unanticipated total, so he rescans his invisible digits once more, somehow convincing himself that this new number must be the right one. "Well, I'll be," he says, to no one in particular. "That ought to fix it, though." He works another quick calculation before speaks again.

I hate to admit it, but he's got both of us lured in now, what with him poking numbers that only he can see out of the clear blue sky—all from the space set roughly seven-and-a-half inches past the end of his nose, right at eye level, to be exact—I didn't feel so bad when a couple of those drywall guys came walking up from the stairwell, both watching Bubba intently as he jabs numbers into the air. Until, that is, the elder of the two spots something amiss, raises a fuss as approaches, and is soon right beside Bubba, pointing out the error he found, someplace there in the clearness that is now their shared workspace. The new man's numbers prompt a completely unexpected debate between the two, both now prattling away in what think is Spanish.

I squint my eyes a little harder and crane my neck, trying to see if I've missed something that those two are both now pointing at. The older Mexican fellow gets really wound up about something in the computation. Bubba stands back, listening carefully. I don't see a damn thing, but just to be certain, I pull out a handkerchief and wipe the lens of my safety glasses clean. By the time I put them back on my nose, the Mexican seems to be bringing Bubba over to his way of thinking, whatever that is. Bubba nods slowly as he considers the revised totals.

"Ooooooh," Bubba says. "Good eye. I never would have seen that, *Gracias!*"

"No problem," the other man says, without so much as an accent.

Wait a minute. How did—Bubba shuts it down before we can put too much more brainpower into this elaborate rouse his buddy Fernando is helping him create.

"Hey kid," he says, the boy stopping his video and stuffing his phone in a pocket before he can refocus on the fellow up the ladder. Bubba juts his chin toward the far wall. "Could you grab that big, orange-handled tool from my box over there?"

The kid, given a mission, lit right up and pranced like a baby deer over to Bubba's big green box. He rummages through its contents for several minutes, head down, skinny ass up in the air. Bubba, meanwhile, climbs down the ladder and measures the *correct* dimensions for his walls. Just before he makes his cuts, the kid chimes up.

"Orange handle, you say?" he says, voice echoing inside the box.

"Dadgumit!" Bubba says, snapping his fingers. "I almost

forgot. I loaned it to the electricians earlier this week. Why don't you go grab it from them? Tell them I sent you to get my board stretcher."

That kid trots right for me.

"Don't suppose you know who borrowed Bubba's board stretcher, do you?" he asks.

I ain't gonna lie. I had a hard time keeping a straight face. Bubba doubled over laughing back there in my line of sight sure didn't help any. "Let me see," I say, imagining endless checkout lanes, crippled puppies, webcam hemorrhoid surgery footage—anything at all, really—just to keep that shit-eating grin off my face.

"I think it was Larry," I say. "But I can't be sure he's still got it. He's a good start, anyway. I think he's on the . . . sixth floor today . . . yeah, why don't you go check with him?"

Now, let's ignore the fact we're in the basement and I just sent this kid up seven flights of stairs. Let's ignore, too, that Larry remembered Chuck using that board stretcher last, and sent him back down another four flights. Or that Chuck, upon hearing why he needed such a fool thing, decided another fellow had an even better tool for the job:

"Go find Jamal," he tells him. "He was up on the roof yesterday, but he's the *only* one who has what you need. Tell him Chuck said to let you use his a 14-inch *pantalón* snake." Then he grabbed him by his shoulders, got right in his face and looked him dead in his eye. "This part is critical," he adds, not even a hint of a smile. "It's gotta be the fourteen-incher. Anything smaller just won't do."

That kid spent the better part of the afternoon on this snipe hunt before the big boss finally sent him home. He gave us all a stern talking to at the next safety meeting. The dangers of pranking somebody on a jobsite or some such.

Bubba and I couldn't have cared less. We were both still a little drunk from the night before but well on our way to becoming fast friends.

"Ever heard of the Gorgenheim Girls?" I wasn't sure if I had. But that's the first question Bubba sprang on me to defend his good name on that whole Playmate thing. If his intent was to throw me off by asking such a random question, it worked.

He had a knack for stuff like that. A natural born con-man, if ever there was. Course, this whole Playboy thing came at the tail end of what turned out to be a two-and-a-half-hour-long phone call. He had a knack for stuff like that, too: Blabbering on and on about not a damn thing until you physically needed a nap. I was driving back from one of our recently finished jobs out in West Texas. I was captive, for the moment. If nothing else, it made those dull ass miles pass a little quicker, I suppose.

"They was this cabaret act back in the vaudeville days," he tells me. "Used to be pretty big up north. Chicago, Philadelphia, New York, places like that. I had to Google them, myself . . ."

"You did *what* to them?"

"I'm getting to that—*holy shit*, man. That's that chick I was telling you about. The one who lives down there on the corner—you remember—good girls bend at the knee and bad girls bend all night long? Well, there she is, man . . . *Damn!*"

"You do realize I'm on the phone, *right?*"

"Your loss, man," he says.

That's another one of Bubba's knacks: I don't care if she's seventeen or seventy-five, he's gonna gawk. I don't care if he's writing a eulogy or telling you the delicate details about passing his latest kidney stone, a chick walks by and he goes all labra-doodle spotting a squirrel.

"Well anyway, my neighbor had this big garage sale over there where that fine ass chick is bent in half right now—you gotta see this shit, I tell you what; I do believe she's an exhibitionist, man. She regularly opens all her curtains when she takes her showers. Pisses her ol' man off something fierce—I know," he reassures me. "I've got binoculars . . . What was I saying?"

"Googling Gorgenheim Girls."

"Oh yeah—sorry, I get distracted—anyway, they had this big garage sale last weekend. You know that sumbitch made seven thousand dollars from that one day? I been thinking about having one myself, get rid of some of Momma's old stuff. You know, all them angels and doilies and crap. Probably wouldn't bring seven thousand dollars but it'd get it the fuck outa my house. Still, I don't wanna pay that goddamn city permit fee. Can you believe this little shit town makes you get a permit to have a garage sale?"

"Holy *shit*, dude! Does this story have a point?"

"Good things come to those who wait, man. I think that's in the Bible. Besides, you forget, I grew up out there. You told me where you was wallago. I know there ain't shit for at least another thirty miles."

"Won't make that mistake again."

"So, yeah, I thought I'd mosey on over there, see if they had anything worth looking at. Found me some great fishing tackle—got us a good long-handled net, a whole bucket of weights, even a couple of Penn reels I'm gonna tinker with and see if I can't get them back up and operational."

"Cool," I say, hoping he finds his way back to the beaten path again soon. I can't help thinking of that dumbass kid, all those years ago. 'Ol Bubba's got *me* right where he wants me.

". . . So while I'm there, this little old blue-hair walks over from down the street. I figure she's the new neighbor. Saw all sorts of moving trucks and such over there, a few days back. I keep on rummaging about, but I figure this will be as good a time as any to make my acquaintance . . ."

Now me, I can go days without saying a word to another living soul. Just the way I am. Not Bubba. No sir. He could be lost in the Mojave and somehow find the only other bastard in a hundred miles, strike up a conversation, and suddenly know their whole life story, especially if she has tits.

". . . So, she walks around a while, looking at this and that, and spots this exercise bench—sort of like a weight bench, but without the weights—it's got this place to put your feet to do sit-ups and such. You can even adjust the height, you know?"

"Yeah," I'm not even half listening at this point. I slow down and honk my horn at a circle of buzzards on the road. Looks like somebody smeared an eight-pointer last night. From the looks of it, they probably needed some body work, too, after that one.

Bubba tells me she wound up buying that old exercise bench, which he used as his opportunity to introduce himself. She seemed to be struggling with the size of that thing as she made her way back up the street. Bubba can't stand to see anyone struggling with something when he's standing there, not doing a damn thing, especially not some little old lady.

". . . You know me," he says. "I figure it's as good a time as any to make my hellos. So, I ask her, 'You need a hand with that?'"

"Sure, darling," she says. Bubba straightaway latches onto the bench she bought.

"It ain't heavy at all," he says. "I feel right off that the wood on this thing is almost half rotted out already. That sumbitch! He ought to be ashamed of himself, selling something like that to one of his neighbors. And a little old lady, no less. Must've had this thing sitting out his yard or something. What would he have done if she'd fallen and broke a hip or something?"

I stay as silent as I can. I mean, how the fuck would I know the answer to something like that. More importantly, who the fuck cares? If one of my neighbors sued another one of my neighbors, I doubt seriously either would ever tell me about it. Even if they did, I sure as hell couldn't give a damn. I got enough of my own problems to worry with without poking my nose around everybody else's who lives near me. I make a point of not pestering people where I live in hopes they take the hint. That's worked pretty good for me, so far. Way I see it, no need to fuck up a perfectly good system now. Guess that's why folks either think Bubba either hung the moon, or he's a complete ass. Positively, no middle ground anyplace, whatsoever. Hell, if I dropped dead, out in the yard tomorrow, ain't none of *my* neighbors even knows me well enough to feel one way or the other about it.

"Once she gets to talking, you better hang on, man, because that woman couldn't talk more of a blue streak if she were part Smurf."

Hearing that assessment, coming from his lips, it's all I can do to keep from laughing, right out loud. Kinda like the pot calling the crystal meth an abused drug, if you ask me.

She told ol' Bubba all about her recent move and how nice it is to finally be back near where she grew up. No matter how he tries, though, Bubba can't shake the image of all that rotten wood on the lady's new bench.

"As she's telling me about something, I can't help myself," he says. "I roll that bench over to have a look at its bottom side. It's worse than I imagined. I can literally flick it apart with fingernail. Sorry bastard! I hope he shits himself to death, selling crap like that to his neighbors. Well anyway, I show her what I've found, how bad off that wood was. Then I tell her it wouldn't be no trouble at all to fix it for her."

"Really?" I could say damn near anything at this point and he'd never be the wiser. I thought before of making me a recording reel of useless responses for moments just like this one. Always worries me though, he'd figure it out somehow and I'd never hear the end of it. He lost me somewhere about garage sale, but once he gets going, it's a lot easier just to let him talk. He gets all ass hurt if you try for the Readers' Digest version to any story he tells.

". . . She lights right up, at first, but then she starts sidewinding on me. Starts going on and on about how she didn't want to put me out in any way. It's no big deal, I tell her, so she finally agrees to let me fix it. She points out her house—right where all the moving trucks had been, a few days earlier—she tells me she'll be back in a day or two to pick it up and we go our separate ways . . ."

"Mmm hmmm . . ." I check my truck's navigation. Fourteen more miles to the next pit stop. Hope I have enough gas to make it.

". . . So, I take it in my shop, pull the cushions and get to work. That wood was completely rotted out, man. Let me tell you. I toss that hunk of crap in the burn pile and look through my wood samples for a good replacement piece. I find this gorgeous piece of pecan wood about three inches thick. I'd planned to use it as mantel piece at some point, but it's almost the perfect size for this thing, you know? So, I take me a couple measures and start trimming it to size. It'll add some weight to it, but it definitely ain't gonna break on her. Time I get done with it, she'll have to decide which great-grandchild she wants to will the damn thing to . . ."

The gas station sign finally appears on my horizon. Thank God! I wasn't sure how much more of this story I could handle without swerving into oncoming traffic.

"Sounds good, man," I say. "Look, I gotta go. I'm running on fumes, and that's the first gas station I've seen in like two hundred miles. I'll talk to ya later . . ."

"I see how it is," Bubba says. "You don't wanna hear my Playboy Bunny story. That's alright. See if I ever—"

"Yeah OK, dude. I gotta get." Click. *Finally.*

I flick on my blinker, glad I'll finally get to stretch my legs some. I may even enjoy some peace and quiet for the first time since I climbed behind the wheel. Foremost, however,

I needed to inspect their "ultra-clean bathrooms" for leaks, because if it didn't have one already, I definitely had one I was willing to drop off in its place.

I pull back on the highway with only two hundred fifty more miles to go. I've got a full gas tank, an empty bladder and a fresh cup of coffee. Life doesn't get much better than that. I can already feel the sheets of my own bed calling my name. Took us seven whole months to finish that last job—a full month ahead of schedule—and I'm looking forward to a few days of down time before we start it all over again, someplace else. I flip through the radio stations—Tejano, Tejano, Jesus, Tejano—not a damn thing on in this part of the world. And if I listen to that George Strait album one more time, I think I'll jump out of the truck. Only so many of those you can hear without them all starting to sound the same. No wonder ol' George chose to retire, a few years back.

I switch off the radio. Silence it is. I adjust my rearview, set my cruise control and take a long, slow sip off my coffee. About the time I set it back down, my phone rings.

"B&B Construction. How can I help you today?"

". . . So, I get it all cleaned up and put back together, better than if it was new, and I carry it over to her house," Bubba says, as if he'd only paused for a breath rather than said a whiny farewell forty-five minutes ago. Despite traffic being scarce on the highway, the entire Texas population was gathered at the last stop. It took forever to pee and buy a cup of Joe.

". . . I knock on her door and I hear her shuffling around inside. Her head pops up in the curtains. She spots me and goes to the door—man, she must have like a billion locks because all I hear is *thunk, cachunk, click, swipe*—you can tell she's still accustomed to those to the apartments in New York City.

"Come in, come in," she says. "I never expected you so soon."

"I barely get the bench wedged in the door," Bubba says, "and she's already halfway across the room, toting this enormous goblet of wine . . ."

I grab my coffee cup and slump back in my seat, arm draped over the top of the steering wheel. Silence ain't in the cards for me today, apparently.

"You care for a nip?" the old lady asks him before she disappears around the corner.

"Shit man, it's barely ten o'clock in morning," he says, "but I don't want to seem rude either. Before I can say a thing, I hear her pouring me a glass already. Sure, I tell her. She's already coming back, a big ol' glass in each hand now."

"I drink me a bottle of wine every day," she tells Bubba. "Sometimes I even have more than one. Keeps you limber."

Then she winked at him, Bubba swore, but that was only the beginning of his truly strange and twisted afternoon. "I'm sitting there, trying to take a few pulls off this wine glass so I don't spill it everywhere," Bubba says. "She filled that thing smooth to the top, you know. That's when she leans in on me then, straight out of nowhere.

"Drink up, darlin," she says. "We're gonna loosen you up yet." Then she winks again.

"You don't say," I reply, back on my play reel of useless responses.

". . . Now it's kinda dark in this room I just got in. I told you she moved like a week ago, right? I was kinda expecting boxes and shit all over the place. But no. It's like she's lived there all her life. She's got magazines spread out on her end tables, books and knickknack's all over her shelves, and pictures hung on every wall. Hell, I don't have that much shit about, and I've been in my place for 25 years now . . ."

"Hmmm." I say, taking another sip.

Next thing he knows, Bubba says the woman sets her glass down, grabs that workout bench from him like it's a box of Kleenex, and hauls it off to the other room.

"Make yourself at home," she calls back. "Have a seat . . ."

He pauses there. Sounds like he's still trying to finish that glass of wine she gave him two days ago. He ain't much of a drinker.

". . . Now I'm still standing by the door, kind of floored she took that bench off as quick as she did. That pecan plank I used probably weighed a good sixty pounds by itself. Well, I figure what the hell, and I start making my way a little deeper into the room. Like I said, it's kind of dark in there, so my eyes are still adjusting from outside. That's when I start noticing these pictures she has all over her walls, though. It's literally a who's who of celebrities in there, a lot of them even have autographs . . ."

"Really?" I say, not feigning interest for the first time since this call began. Bubba knows I'm a history and pop culture buff. "Like who?"

". . . There's one of Mickey Mantle. Charlton Heston. Sinatra. Johnny Carson. The Beatles. Trumann Capote. Even LBJ and Nixon. Plus, there's a shitload more I couldn't make out. I mean every wall in this place has got somebody famous on it, and there's dozens of pictures on every wall . . ."

"Wow."

". . . Yeah, but that's only half of it," he says: "In every one of these pictures is this drop-dead *gorgeous* woman. I'm talking pinup girl quality. Just waves of blonde hair, perfect tits and a smile you'd die for, and she's not wearing much more than a tiara in most of those shots."

He's standing there, checking out the photographs, when all at once, the woman appears out of nowhere, immediately behind him. "I see you've spotted my pictures," she says . . .

He pauses, right when this finally got interesting. "*And?*" I say.

". . . Well, I didn't hear her walk up," he says. "I kind of jump a little because she surprised me, and that's when I hear her laughing at me."

"We're just gonna have to loosen you up a bit there, sonny," she says, following her statement up firm but generous pinch on his backside.

"What?" I ask.

"She gooses me . . ."

"No shit?"

". . . Yeah, man. Serious to God! I'm talking full on palm to ass cheek. Now she's really laughing at me because she may have made me jump when she surprised me, but I'm pretty sure I come clean off the floor when she goosed me. You want to make a fat man move, just goose him real good one day . . ."

I couldn't help but laugh.

". . . Yuk it up, buddy! I'd like to see how you would respond when some old broad decides to make you her Man Candy for the day . . ."

"Man Candy," I say, when I finally catch my breath. "That's rich!"

". . . That's *Mister* Man Candy, to you . . ."

Over the next several miles, Bubba filled me in on the woman's history. How she got her start with the Gorgenheim Girls in Chicago when she was only sixteen. How that launched her modeling career and landed her in New York City. How she wound up meeting all the famous folk she had on her walls. How she even started pulling out albums with hundreds more pictures than her walls could hold. And things truly got weird that day.

"I was quite the dish, wasn't I?" she asks Bubba.

"I can't let her down," he says, "and honestly, she really *was*. Hell yeah, I told her, her eyes just glittering. I'm trying to be polite and all, but this ol' gal keeps climbing up on me. I'm starting to get a little nervous, you know? I don't wanna be rude, so I figure I'll finish my drink and suddenly remember I left my stove on or something . . ."

"Right," I say.

"Well, I'm flipping through these pictures and come across one that looks like the same chick on the walls standing next to this dude in a smoking jacket with a cigar. Is that Hugh Heffner? I ask her."

"Oh yeah," she says, from the next room. She was working on another wine cork and walks back out with a fresh bottle. "I was a Playboy Centerfold through most of the seventies," she says. "I *lived* at Hugh's mansion for several years."

"No shit," I say.

"Yeah," Bubba tells me. "Well, I'm listening to her tell her story and what-not, but the whole time she's talking she keeps throwing all these innuendos my way, you know? Nearly everything she says has two meanings—aww, what's the word I'm thinking?—"

"Double entendre."

"Yeah, that's it. ON-Tonder. . . Well, she keeps tossing it out there, right? And she keeps filling my glass. I finally ask her—you know, you never know how to go about that sort of thing with an older lady—but I ask her outright: How old are you anyway? You know what she tells me?"

"No, I don't."

"*Eighty!*" Bubba says. "She just had her *eightieth* birthday up in New York before she moved down here. Now I'm really floored. I wouldn't have put her a day over sixty myself. I mean, she gets around so well and she has this—I don't know—worldly way about her, I guess, that you don't expect from somebody that just turned eighty. And like I said wallago, all that ontonder and what-not. Like when she took the album from me. I wasn't halfway through it yet and she reached over and grabbed it out my hands. Mind you, almost every photo in that thing has her standing there naked as the day she was born. . ."

"I better put this up before something comes up that it's

gonna take us all afternoon put back down," she tells Bubba, eyeing him with this wicked little grin on her face.

"This chick is laying it all out there," Bubba says. "I mean, she really wants some—"

"What's she doing living there?" I interrupt.

"That's the thing," Bubba says. "One of her daughters wound up marrying one of these ranchers around here. She lived in New York for a long time, but she's getting up in years and got diagnosed with dementia a few years back. She's still in the early stages of it, but she decided to move a little closer to her family, just the same . . ."

"Hmmm."

"Well, anyway, this chick wants me, man," Bubba says. "And she keeps putting it out there, the whole time. She even offers to give me a tour of the place, wants to show me her bedroom, which she says everyone should see at least once. I tell you, man, I don't know if it's the wine or what, but I'm looking at her—she's wearing one of those swishy, old lady jogging suits, but ol' girl's still got her shape—I just can't get my head around the fact she's eighty . . ."

"Come on, dude!" I say. "Take one for the team! When's somebody like you ever gonna say he got to bed a Playboy Bunny?"

"What you trying to say there, buddy?"

"Well, what happened?"

"I was a gentleman," Bubba says. "I finished my glass and went back home."

"Yeah, right. I'm calling bullshit once again."

"That's my story and I'm sticking to it."

It took about another hour to get him to hang up, but with San Antonio steadily filling my windshield, I managed to part ways. He knew I hated driving in that town, so he finally agreed to hang up. At least the radio offerings got better for the remainder of my ride. All the way, though, I couldn't get over this bullshit story he tossed at me for the bulk of my drive home.

The things he thinks up sometimes . . . Like I said, it takes a bit of salt.

Despite having talked with him for nearly the last four hours, I somehow managed to keep a lid on the one surprise I was carrying. Because we finished the job a month ahead of schedule, the contractor awarded us a ten-thousand-dollar bonus, all cash, all under the table. I figured I'd swing by Bubba's place and drop off his share before I got home.

As I turn onto his block, my jaw drops so hard it feels unhinged. There, sitting on the steps of that ratty ol' trailer of his, is a little old lady, bottle of wine in one hand and massive wineglass in the other.

Bubba's grinning like a shit-fed possum as I step out of the truck.

"I'd like you to meet my neighbor, Susanna Scott," he says. "Susie, my business partner and best friend . . ."

The old lady reaches over and pats his thigh.

"Oooo!" she says, eyes glittering like diamonds. "You didn't tell me it was gonna be a *ménage á trois*. No worries. Not my first . . ."

She holds out her withered hand to me.

"Call me Susie," she says. "I'm the Playmate I'm sure you've heard all about by now."

Bad Blood

Why he went to that damn party, Raymond never could quite explain. He asked himself that exact question a million times or more in years since, things turning out like they did. The closest he ever came to a real answer always had something to do with seeing Caleb again.

At one time, you see, he and Caleb were tight as new socks. Inseparable. That was in grade school. Quite a while ago now.

They were strangers now. Nobody anyone would mistake for friends. Not anymore. Raymond worked at dodging him at first, in those first few months, but their paths barely crossed anymore. Life pulled them separate ways. Raymond would never forget the last time he saw him, though—there by the monkey bars in fifth grade, when Caleb pounded his eyes shut, then turned, calm and slow, and walked away. He's never looked back since.

So, why he went to the party was anybody's guess. His reasons were flimsy, at best, Raymond's quick to admit. A bit stalkerish, even. Pitiful with a capital-P.

But Caleb was about the closest thing to a friend Raymond ever had, despite how things turned out between them. It was time to let bygones be, Raymond would later say, to bury the old hatchet, so to speak.

Unless, of course, that phrase involved an actual tool.

That's never good.

✜✜✜

He came to town back in first or second grade—Raymond couldn't remember the exact details anymore—but Caleb approached Raymond on the playground one day, the cold steel of those monkey bars looming there at their backs, the new kid at school and the outcast, who momentarily shared the same status.

"Hi," Caleb said. "What's your name?"

"Raymond," he replied. "And hullo. You're Caleb, right?"

The other boy bobbed his head up and down. Raymond remembered from the entire welcome-to-class rigmarole in homeroom, first thing that morning. "Where'd you come from again?"

"Am'rillo. My mom and me moved here just last night. We lived all sorts of places, 'fore that. There was Oklahoma City. Stillwater. Topeka. Missouri City. Them last two was in Kansas. Mom always giggles when she says we're not in Kansas anymore. I'm not sure why . . ."

Raymond shifted, eyes on the ground, unsure what to say next. That was far more answer than he could've dreamt of. Besides, he'd never heard of most of those places, much less ever been to any of them. Caleb could've just as well listed Neverland and Mordor for all Raymond knew of the map. He'd spent his whole life in the few blocks that was Concrete, Texas, for better or worse.

Caleb didn't seem to notice in the least. He was soon digging in the deep pockets of his new Husky jeans.

"Wanna play cars?" he asked, palming a brown Fall Guy pickup truck and bright orange General Lee.

"Sure," Raymond said, and the two boys were soon on their knees, carving roads in the dirt. One couldn't be seen without the other after that. They were always together, even staying the night at each other's places.

Although Caleb stayed over at Raymond's house a couple of times, far and away the bulk of the two boys' time was spent over at Caleb's house. For one, he had better toys. Most of the time, too, they were free to do as they pleased at Caleb's place, be it eat ice cream whenever or watch TV to all hours. But far and away, Caleb's mom was unlike anyone he'd ever met, especially as far as mom's went.

"Closed doors lead to closed minds," she said often. And she practiced what she preached, every night as she got ready for her graveyard shift at the café. Caleb's mom was pretty— like *seriously hot* pretty—like Wonder Woman in a business skirt, each time she slid into her uniform. Reflections of her, back arched, would dance across his daydreams well into Raymond's adulthood—those tiny, silky bands of alluring black and eye-catching blood red lace gliding like half-melted ice cubes across all that lovely curvy, flawless skin—they stayed forever etched on his heart.

"I can't stand a closed door," she'd say. "Closed doors lead to closed minds."

And Raymond fought lion-hearted to expand his mind exponentially, especially at her house when she would get ready for her graveyard shift at the roadside café. He asked her one day if she served zombies or monsters or witches or just ghosts. She sounded such whimsy, inhibition, and smoky joy in her laugh.

"Darlin,' I think you just described my whole section on any given night," she said, laughing again. The boy laughed with her, too, but had no idea why.

"Oh God," she'd say then. "They're gonna fire my ass if come in late again." Then she fluffed up her hair and touched up her wine-red lips with her pinkie. "Kisses boys," she'd call out, and bending down only part of the way needed, she'd smooch the air above them so as not foul her meticulous makeup—"Muah! Muah!"—then quick as she floated in, she dashed off again, into the night. "Y'all be good," she'd holler back, "Don't stay up all night!" And left them there, alone, barely seven, with *Twilight Zone* marathons and visions of Linda Carter, mostly naked, dancing vivid in his mind.

Despite how things turned out, those were still some of the best memories Raymond ever had. But even the best of times end, eventually. And Raymond had a knack for learning things the hard way. Some fellows are good at sports; others excel at math. Raymond's specialty came in the form of naïveté. Having grown up sheltered like he did—*Sesame Street* was too elicit for his house, his mother always said, "full of tramps doing inappropriate things with dolls"—he had no life experience to help stay him away from the hassles most folks simply avoid. He just knew no better.

Maybe he simply needed to see how the other half lived—all those popular people with their popular cars parked at their popular houses, talking popular words about their popular clothes, while popular crowds admired their popular haircuts, barely heard over the popular bands belting out popular tunes on the popular sound systems. Such full lives. What *FUN* it all seemed.

No wonder they constantly told him to *F*-off. He sucked all the life from their *FUN*, as most *UN*-remarkable, *UN*-interesting, *UN*-populars tend to do.

Just one night. Just once before he graduated, before he packed his stuff and got the hell gone. To anyplace. The hell out of there, mostly. But just once, he'd get to see how everyone else lived. Who could've guessed that experience might outlive them both? No doubt, the stories about what happened would, anyway.

Outlast them, that is. That much was certain.

+⸈+ +⸈+ +⸈+

Raymond couldn't say he knew what all happened back then. He certainly didn't understand it, anyhow. Not then, particularly. Even as a senior, he still had a few questions. But Caleb's mom, a waitress over at the local truck stop back then, apparently got wrapped up in some scandal with Riley Richardson, this bigtime oilman who lived there in town.

Raymond remembered the church elders talking about it, not long after it happened. Apparently, Mrs. Richardson, Riley's wife at the time, came home early one day and found Caleb's mom in her bed. A neighbor who witnessed the whole thing through open blinds later testified at trial that Mrs. Richardson left her husband and Caleb's mom in the bedroom to their "activities" as she walked, slow and calm, back to the kitchen, where she grabbed a butcher knife from a drawer, washed and dried it, and then returned to the bedroom. She even waited for them to finish up before she attacked, slashing away at both Caleb's mom and her husband with the sharp, freshly washed blade. Put them both in the hospital, and landed Mrs. Richardson a lengthy stay behind bars, from what Raymond heard.

What truly confused the boy, however, was that for as grim as reports were about his friend's mother, there were almost as many people laughing about what happened as there were people gossiping about it. One night after service, for instance, this one group of men at the back of the church could hardly keep a straight face as they made cracks about Old Man Riley never quite measuring up again, or that he'd only be half the man he used to be. Those men laughed so hard tears fell from their eyes.

It would be years before Raymond even understood their jokes. Even then, he failed to see what they found so damn funny. It sounded plumb awful to him.

They said something else, too, that would puzzle Raymond for years. He barely made it out, what with the men at the back of that church barely able to breathe between their fits of laughter, but it basically boiled down to this: If Old Man Riley was really feeling bad about what happened, he could just buy Caleb's mom some brand-new tits. After all, he'd already paid for "plenty of upgrades on other floozies in town," they said.

That one could buy a boob was news to Raymond, though where one would go to pick one up was anyone's guess. He certainly never saw that shelf at the Walmart. Apart from logistics, though, Raymond also couldn't wrap his head around *why* Caleb's mom would want them. She already had her a set—a fairly nice one, if he was any judge—he was certain on that part. Of course, he'd heard about the other woman with the knife, too. Maybe she'd damaged them somehow, like scratched them up somehow or, worse still, deflated them somehow. Could a boob pop like a balloon? Raymond didn't know. And would it hurt if it did?

He certainly couldn't bring such questions to his mother. He'd've never gotten rid of the soap flavor on his tongue if he had. So, he was left to his own devices. The library was no help. The librarian kicked him out when he asked her how to spell *floozie*. And while the tit thing left enough mysteries to fill a book for him, the whole notion that one could possibly "upgrade them," as they put it, simply baffled him.

They sure found it funny as hell, though. And that's about the time his mother chose to walk up, far less than pleased at finding her boy eavesdropping on conversations like that. At church, no less. She gave those men a good what-for, completely ruining any future possibility he might have of them clarifying their statements so that Raymond might better grasp their meaning. Then, she snatched the boy and dragged him home. Although he hadn't spoken a word of it, he still wound up sucking soap when he got home.

Not that it calmed his mother down any, not her yanking him by the ear the whole time, the entire walk home, nor that hour he sat there with that blue bar of Dial dissolving on his tongue. Not in the least. If anything, it only got her going, Raymond was certain.

She was smooth *pissed*, though he still couldn't say he understood why. She kept fussing at him about how he brought such filth into her house. How he brought shame on their whole family. She made him scrub the entire house clean, whipped him with a belt whenever he wasn't moving fast enough for her liking. She kept him home from school for three whole days—scrubbing and whipping, whipping and scrubbing—when she finally let him go back to school, she wouldn't leave until she found that "no-account friend of his" and listened as Raymond ended it, right then and there. Then and only then would she leave, in her paper-thin Mumu, the pink and green plastic curlers making her head seem like some sort of strange Picasso painting, with all its neon pastels and unnatural lumps sprouting everywhere. She dragged him across campus by his ear until they spotted Caleb. Then, she stood there and waited until she'd witnessed the deed done.

Raymond caught up with Caleb, later that day, apologizing profusely for what his mother made him do. Caleb's eyes filled with bitter tears as he spat the venom right back.

"I didn't do nothing to nobody, but everybody acts like it was my fault, somehow. I didn't even know Momma knew the guy, and now she's in the hospital, hooked to all these machines. Some nurse there said she might die, and it would serve her right for what she done. She's all I got, man. I don't care if she did do something she shouldn't."

Raymond tried to console his friend.

"I heard the church elders talking about it," he said. "They said she was sleeping in his bed. She was probably just tired from work."

Caleb stared at Raymond, his mouth hanging open. It was the kind of look Raymond would've expected if he'd just grabbed a warm dog turd off the ground, ate half of it, then smeared the rest on Caleb's face. Sans turds, however, Raymond wasn't sure what prompted it. He stood there, blinking back at his friend.

"Are you retarded or something?" Caleb said. "I can't believe you're really that fucking stupid."

Raymond froze. He didn't know what to do. They were just fourth graders, after all. Neither had even dropped an F-bomb yet. Not at school, especially. You didn't even hear older kids say stuff like that. Not back then, that's for sure.

"Know what? I didn't need this shit today," Caleb said. "'Specially not from you. Fuck your apology, and fuck you, too."

As if to punctuate what he'd said, Caleb hocked back and fired an enormous loogie at Raymond's forehead. It covered his entire left eye in warm spittle.

Caleb got two weeks of detention for that, one for his cursing and another for spitting. He only spoke to Raymond once more after that, a couple weeks after, when he finally got out of detention. It wasn't much of conversation, though. He caught up with Raymond on the playground, that same place by the monkey bars where'd they first made each other's acquaintance. The same place where so many of the other, bigger boys had throttled them both so many times before.

"Hey, you sorry son-of-a-bitch," was all he said.

Then he pounced on Raymond. Caleb wasn't nearly as big as the other kids that had pounded on them both in that very same spot, but Raymond remembered it hurting much worse. Caleb wasn't trying to just hurt or bully Raymond. Instead, he fought with the jagged edges of his shattered heart. He wanted to leave Raymond marked, just like Old Man Riley's wife had left him and his mom, both.

Still feeling guilty about publicly renouncing his friend, Raymond didn't even try to defend himself.

He just took his beating. He figured he'd earned it.

He owed him that much, at least.

Not that it would've done him much good. Caleb had stockpiled miles of rage, fueled by all the whispers around town about his mom. Two weeks in the hole for spitting on him sure didn't help, either. Caleb focused every wrong, every misguided comment, and every bit of anger he could muster and channeled it to his fists. He climbed up on Raymond's chest and swung with both fists, over and over, until he'd beaten Raymond unconscious. Then, he just kept on pounding him, over and over, leaving his face a bloody mess until one of the coaches finally pulled Caleb off him. Thank God he did. Raymond was certain he'd be pounding on him still if he hadn't.

When Raymond came to, later that day in the nurse's office, she told him that she'd had to super glue two of the holes in his face to stop the bleeding. The one above his left eye ran nearly the entire length of his eyebrow, which opened shortly before Raymond blacked out. It filled his entire eye socket with blood. The second spot on his face must've come open after he was out. Formed this wicked, ragged letter X, right below that same eye, just above his cheekbone. About two inches wide and an inch-and-a-half tall.

The cut across the eyebrow never healed just right. It left that whole side of his face with a noticeable droop. At least the scar was mostly hidden by his eyebrow, however, even if it did cause his brow to grow in kinda wonky. Both the droopy eye and wonky eyebrow only added to Raymond's serial-killer-in-training look. That big X on his cheek would remain the rest of his days, just as raw and red as the day he got it. It wouldn't show up for a couple years still, but it was about the only plus to the rashy, red acne beard that took up residence on his face—at least with a fresh bloom of pimples constantly cropping up every few days he didn't have that big jagged red X staring back at him from every mirror.

That night, however, his whole face throbbed, as those cuts swelled to the size of oranges. The next morning, his whole head was nearly twice its normal size, and both eyes were swollen mostly shut. Although his mother let him stay home that day, she refused to give him so much as an aspirin for the pain or swelling. He would walk around with purple-black eyes for an entire month afterward. But no one felt sorry for him. Not at school, and most definitely, not at home. "I told you to stay away from that no-account punk," his mother said. "But you didn't listen to me, did you?"

Both now older, of course, Caleb and his mom finally made it, when she married his new dad. She was an even cooler mom, Raymond heard from others at school. She was one of those *buy-you-a-new-pickup-for-Christmas* sorts of moms, one of them *let-me-buy-you-a-keg-for-your-house-party* sorts of moms, one of those *here's-a-box-of-rubbers-cuz-I-don't-want-you-knocking-up-one-of-those-little-twits-you-always-have-around* sorts of moms. Just like Wonder Woman, too, she got better with age, Raymond also heard. She was doing something called *yoga* now (whatever that was). All he knew about it now was that she wore nothing but skin-tight clothes (something called *a Leo-Pard*? His mind danced with spots) as she slowly and deliberately twisted herself in knots. He even heard somebody say that Caleb's new dad *had* sprung for a new set of boobs. What really stumped him, though, was what they did with the old pair.

Caleb's mom was nothing like his own, though she used to be far softer and slimmer and more maternal, back when Caleb came around. These days, she lazed round like the big blob she was, dressed in threadbare rags like a street bum. While other moms were doling out free beer kegs and trucks, his was digging through charity bins at the Pentecostal church, dressing him in dead man's clothes from entire other eras.

It's true: That's when she especially wanted to go through those bins—whenever one of those old codgers from the church finally died. It might be a few weeks, sometimes even months or years, but sooner or later, one of the man's kids would finally show up, either to move into his house or sell it outright. Then, it never failed, the countdown fell to hours before they'd drop off the dead guy's clothes at the church.

Only thing Raymond could figure was they were just too embarrassed to drive clean out of town to the dump with a load like that. He couldn't blame them.

Just imagine the type of lunatic people might think you were if you broke down someplace and it was discovered the Great Gatsby and all his guests had stripped down to their undergarments in your car. Or the cast of Hee Haw just started heaping all their duds in bundles at you. And not the cool stuff like Grandpa Jones, the washtub tramps or the guy who did the KORN news reports wore. No, that would be too kind. These were like Roy Clark and Buck Owens specials, collars down to their knees and enough polyester to turn the sky ink black for a month if they ever caught fire.

But there'd be his mom, palming every piece, from blown-out socks to oversized tightie whiteys, elastic waist-bands gone, and painted all across their backsides this Jurassic shade of brown. Yep, those were the pieces his mother seemed to love best of all, because you know where all those clothes would wind up? Raymond's closet. She'd pack it so full, he couldn't even walk in.

Don't believe it? Flip through his school photos and find the school's worst-dressed kid. His mother saw to it that he was so dorkily dressed that he would have to move far away when he left. Because there wasn't a girl within a hundred miles who hadn't pointed and guffawed at the pictures, or worse still, delivered their mockery in person, yelling things like, "Who dressed you? Your mom?" All the boy could do was pull his best Droopy the Dog—or who was that donkey that moped around everywhere Winnie the Pooh and Piglet went? That's right, *Eeyore*—in his Howdy Doodie duds and say only the only retort that seemed appropriate, his most defeated-sounding, "Yeah . . ."

And the clothes weren't the worst of it.

He explained it once to Caleb, one of the few times he stayed over there. Raymond scanned the room for signs of his mother and not seeing her, quickly leaned in and blurted it out before she got back. "Whatever you do," he whispered, "never ever let her catch you playing with it—'taking matters into your own hands,' she calls it—you know . . . Down *there* . . . She goes crazy mad if you do. Don't even wash it too long in the bath. She comes unglued. Total—"

"What are you boys whispering about?"

His Mom reappeared. Raymond was mortified, but Caleb saved the day on that one. Sort of . . .

"Raymond was telling me this funny story about a little worm taking a bath," he said. "It was really funny."

Raymond turned beet red, afraid his mother would see straight through it.

"Well, y'all don't need to be whispering like a bunch of thieves," she said. "It's rude. You got something to say, speak up so we all can hear it. Got that?"

"Yes ma'am," came the boys' refrain.

Two things never happened in Raymond's house ever again since the day he came home with his eyes beat shut by Caleb's hand. The first was they never ate pancakes anymore. Not at home. His mother didn't even buy the mix anymore, despite it being one of Raymond's favorite foods. He attributed it to the fact that, when Caleb had been over, probably his second or third time to sleep in their beds, bathe in their tub, and play in their yard, Raymond asked his mom to make pancakes. Caleb liked them so much, she fried up a whole other batch. They became a regular staple whenever he stayed with them. But then, after that beating, they were never around anymore. The other thing he noticed was that Raymond couldn't remember seeing his mother smile ever again. Not that she did much of it before. Not with Raymond, anyway. But they always seemed to come so easily whenever Caleb was there.

Across town, Caleb's life was undergoing some massive life changes as well, Raymond heard through the grapevine at school. He'd gotten expelled for the rest of the year for beating Raymond like he did. There were only two months left in the school year, anyway, and after a couple weeks of summer classes, he got to finish out the year and move on with the rest of his grade. Plus, he had a spot waiting for him on the school football team, playing for the same coach that pulled him off Raymond. He took to the sport eagerly and really excelled at it. They didn't win, but he actually got to go with his team to the state playoff game at Cowboys Stadium in Arlington.

Raymond didn't know shit about football, so he couldn't have told you what position his old friend played. His mother never allowed him to watch such a violent sport on her TV. Not in her house. No sir. Of all her random and ridiculous house rules, especially when it came to the TV, the one about football he never really minded much. Maybe it was the lack of men folk in his life, but nothing about the sport captivated his interest.

Still, he couldn't but feel pride in his friend's accomplishment when he played his game. He even fell asleep listening to it on the radio. He had no idea what was happening in the actual game, based on what the announcers were saying about it—he knew none of the jargon, and everything they said was loaded with it. Mainly, though, he simply listened for Caleb's name, which they said plenty of times before he finally fell asleep, halfway through whatever it was the announcers kept calling overtime play, hooting and hollering like they were at the world national bull riding championships.

Caleb had massive changes brewing on the home front as well, Raymond would learn. Both Old Man Riley and Caleb's mom got out of the hospital in relatively good shape, considering an angry woman had taken a butcher knife to them. They'd probably have some fairly wicked scars they'd wear with them as a constant reminder, not unlike the big red X on his own face. Old Man Riley wasted no time divorcing the woman who cut his pecker off, and no sooner than ink was applied to the divorce decree, he married Caleb's mom and moved them both out to his mansion on the hill, way on the other side of town. Beyond the elevation in status that being on the football team brought him, Caleb and his mom never wanted for anything ever again. In fact, while Raymond was busy haunting pizza places and funeral parlors, trying to secure a cheap ride from one of the drivers, Caleb had just taken delivery of his fourth vehicle: a 1969 fully restored and customized, gunmetal silver Chevy Camaro— one of the toughest looking muscle cars of the whole era—a gift located for him by Old Man Riley, as Caleb wrapped up one stage of life and prepared for the next. That's how the old man said it, he'd heard through his usual eavesdropping on the grapevine. That '69 being a rare collectible, he parked it in his own personal garage, right next to his 1988 Pontiac Firebird T-top, his first car, and the jacked up Ford F-350, his second; and that brand new Harley Fat Boy he got last year, all of them a similar gunmetal and chrome combination like the Camaro.

The hospital apparently reattached Old Man Riley's pecker, too, somehow, because about a year after they wed, Caleb had him a new baby brother. Caleb was on the cusp of finishing high school, but his kid brother was still in second grade.

Yet through it all, Caleb and Raymond hadn't said so much as hello or fuck off to one another the entire time. Eight years had passed since he'd left him laid out there, bleeding in the dirt, unconscious by the monkey bars. He certainly hadn't been invited to their place over on the hill—Rich Boy Row, they had called it with sneers on their faces back when they were friends—but even if they weren't on the outs for the better part for a decade, Raymond wouldn't have gotten an invite. For one, they were in completely different social strata, these days. Dudes like Caleb wouldn't be caught dead with a loser like Raymond.

So, to say the tension lingering midair between them was noticeable the day Raymond showed up, knocking on the front door no one ever used during one his rich-boy parties at his rich-boy digs on the rich-boy side of town, unwelcome and uninvited, was a practice in the fine art of understatement. Caleb's mom, of course, already tipsy from her steady diet of mimosas since some time that morning, did positively nothing to make the boys' reunion any less complicated or strange.

Before he ever got to Caleb, however, Raymond had to get inside the door first. He wouldn't have known the woman who answered the door from Eve. If she'd handed him a photo ID when she answered the door, he wouldn't have believed it. Because this woman looked positively nothing like anyone he remembered, least of all Caleb's mom. For one, her hair was all different. Instead of those long dark luscious locks he remembered, her hair was short, upswept and blonde, like some strange woodland nymph's. Her painted-on clothes were no giveaway either, because apart from that enormous rack she had, a full two letter sizes larger than anything in his memories, she had nothing of that curvaceous pinup girl quality he remembered of Caleb's mom. This woman had the taut, wiry build of a distance runner, which made her look far younger than either of their mom's should have been. For the record, Raymond looked almost nothing like that fresh-faced, cow-licked boy she remembered, either. He'd grown a good two feet taller than he was when she'd last seen him, before that big red X and wonky eyebrow became part of his general features. Instead of that close-cropped hair of his youth, he now kept a shaggy, unkempt appearance, not helped even slightly by the uneven bristle he let grow down each of his cheeks, both ill attempts at hiding the scarlet letter on his face. If anything, it made it all the more noticeable because the wound never sprouted any hair. And while his build was nothing like Caleb's buff, chiseled physique, adolescence and its smarmy brew of hormones had added a layer or three of muscle to his shoulders and neck that had not been there before.

So, there they stood, Raymond and this woman, eyeing each other up and down, like some weird funhouse mirror, each of them somewhat familiar to the other, for some reason, but neither exactly sure why. Perhaps it was something about those sad eyes they both wore, eyes that knew ridicule, for bet-ter or worse. She must've seen it, too, because every time it seemed she'd cracked the puzzle as to the identity of this mys-terious stranger looking back at her, just as the answer seemed right there on the tip of her tongue, she'd pause and rethink the possibilities. Back and forth they went, for three or four minutes solid before either spoke a word. The only noticeable difference between them—aside from one being definitely female, her mountainous mammaries spilling out of the skin-tight top she wore—was that one clearly wanted inside.

At last, the light of recollection flickered on for one of them.

"I remember *YOU*," she said, loud enough for folks on Raymond's side of town to hear.

"God, you're beautiful," Raymond said, the words spill-ing before he could stop them.

So, how'd he end up at that party? Suffice it to say, Raymond would have stood in line for days to endure his own public castration, in all its gore and glimmer, if it meant, finally, he could get away from that awful mother of his.

But he couldn't say that. He couldn't say that to anyone. Nor could he say half the shit he wished he could about Caleb's mom, or, for matter, even Caleb, who he still considered his best friend. Because Caleb, for young Raymond, was the only friend he ever had the boy didn't need to imagine. Even though, one dreary day, right after lunch in late November, out near the monkey bars where the two boys played every day in fourth grade, Caleb savagely leapt on a bewildered Raymond and beat him unconscious. And even then, Caleb didn't stop there; but beat him more still, pounding Raymond's face, two-fisted, until literally, Caleb, finally wore himself out. No longer able to lift his arms, young Caleb finally stood up, flecked head to toe in the blood of yesterday's friend. He stood up, slow and calm, and he turned his back—he turned his back on his friend—and never looked back again.

So, why'd he go to that party? Indeed, the answers were many and terribly complex. Yet at the exact same time, vexing as it may seem, the answers were also far too few. The answer Raymond usually gave: "I can't honestly say." They'd be offered as key evidence at his murder trial and every petition for retrial for years afterward.

Goddamn. I hate talking on these things . . .

Well, shit! Here goes: Now, I'm no one special, of course, just a struggling lawyer trying to manage my practice, best I can, and make enough to keep mine and the ex-wife's mortgages paid, but I thought it then and I still think it's true now. From the first time he fielded that very question on up to now—which is a hellova lot of years, we all know—but before another word was spoken by anyone, before I knew anything else about him, he spoke these words first, in genuine sincerity and truths absolute.

And sad as it sounds, I offered that one shred of evidence upon which I based my entire claim. Unlike many of you, I heard the boy called on to answer that same question, time and again, and no matter how healthy or beaten or sickened he may have been, it was always the same: "I can't honestly say."

No matter how deliberate or broken his mind, heart or spirit, it was the *only* answer he ever gave, the one and only that I ever heard him give.

"I can't honestly say."

I've heard that story so many times I can't help but feel it was my own somehow. Too bad the judge, old senile bastard that he was, just never saw it that way. So, I'll be driving to Huntsville tomorrow. We're trying for a stay from the governor, but we all know what sort of asshole he can be. Just thought I'd touch base, see if maybe you wouldn't wanna come along for the ride and all, ol' Raymond being your first big break and all as county DA.

I still say you have the wrong man, but you and I both know how far that's gotten me after all these years.

Alright, well, I guess you're not in.

I'll see you after, I suppose . . .

Forget the Alamo

No sooner than you get going one direction, life up and backhands you out of nowhere, slaps you around like the whiny bitch you are, and makes you wish it's all just some bad dream.

I couldn't wake up from this nightmare. It just went on and on.

Thankfully, there was Jeremy. He knew how to dream. He never sweated the small stuff—had a knack for sluffing off distractions—kept his eyes focused on some pie-in-the-sky notion of a loftier tomorrow.

Most folks assumed he was just nuts.

I always figured he was one of the last true friends I had left on the planet.

The firings at the *Post* couldn't have caught us more off guard. That was the consensus, anyway. Just days after we did what no one else ever had before—won six Pulitzers in a single year—the office brass called the week's second mandatory powwow.

On Monday, it was all pride and praise. Catcalls and congratulations. Whistles and woohoos. We never could've done something like this—collecting all those nods from the Pulitzer committee—were it not for everyone's valued dedication and attention to detail shown in every single edition we published, every single day of the year. That's what they said. Their precise words. Never in the organization's rich history had they seen a finer team, although *team* didn't truly do us justice. We were more of a *family*, they said with a heavy stress on the final word, because that's the kind of commitment it takes to pull off what we do each day. Then they stopped right there, our undauntable editors, and simply stared at us.

You could've heard a fly fart. Meanwhile, the big bosses, four of them in all, peered slow and intense out into the crowd of faces, all staring back at them. For those closer to the front of this freakshow, I'm sure they were aiming for one of those meaningful eye contact moments, the kind you sometimes see in one of those bullshit inspirational movies about teachers in the barrio or some such. From where I was, it seemed a hellova lot more like the fellow working their teleprompter suddenly dropped dead of a heart attack, and nobody knew what to do next. So, they wandered about, staring at all of us as we stared back at them, for a ridiculously long time. Finally, one of them took mercy on us. One big family, he said, and that room erupted like a boy's boarding school that just learned Hugh Hefner kindly sent along the past year's centerfolds to act as cheerleaders for the debate team.

Well, maybe not *that* exciting. I would've hooted and hollered myself, had the cheerleaders come pom-pomming through the door. As it stood, I barely made it back in time before the whole smoke-blowing session began. I'd been up on the rooftop, you see, blowing a bit of my own smoke. That's where Jeremy and I met most evenings to—um—*prepare* for the next few hours of staring at our computer screens.

Now, I don't know where he got the stuff, but Jeremy always found the best weed in town. Mind you, I don't say such things lightly. Long as I'd known him, and that's going on three decades now, he always has. He's legendary for it.

But right before we would've made our usual climb to the roof, Jeremy's phone rang. He got called to a meeting. He got up to leave and veered my direction on his way out.

Leaning in behind me, he pointed at my computer screen. "Did you see this story?" he asked me. No one ever took up that much of my personal space. Ever. I wasn't sure what to do, exactly. I half-ass nodded, stared where he pointed. In barely a whisper, he said, "See you in a bit," and pulled back, patted my shirt pocket a couple times, right next to my pen, and then he was off. "You need to check that out," he said. "We're going to need to give it some attention." Wasn't until the aroma of the oily green bud wafted up from my pocket that I finally snapped to what happened. By then, Jeremy was nearly out the door. "Go on to lunch without me," he called back. "I'll catch up." And he was gone.

I dug it when we talked in code like that, especially when I figured out that he was.

Although I kept the traditional fires lit, he never showed, so I wound up smoking the whole damn thing by lonesome. Typically, when we came back, there were maybe six people on the entire floor. Counting us. If there was anybody else, it was a writer or two, usually, and most of them wouldn't talk to us if their lives depended on it. We were wire watchers on copy desk, the bottom of the food chain. When we came to work, everyone else was headed home, the day's pages built already, and the presses shooting out newspapers by the tens of thousands Those pages stayed as they were unless something huge and unexpected happened between 8 p.m. and midnight, which happened much less frequently than you might think. Made for some mighty dull evenings, let me tell you. But for slackers like us, you couldn't find a better job. Plus, we got to say we worked for the world-famous *Post*, a fact that got me laid on more than one occasion.

Having smoked an entire joint of some truly primo shit,

all by myself, and walking back into a fully-staffed news-room—everyone waiting for the big bosses to show up—I had some serious ass-pucker happening. I skirted the crowd's outer edges until I wound up beside this huge pillar way in the back. Even then, I kept trying to wedge myself into the cracks in the floor, convinced that everyone who glanced my direction knew I was high as hell. I was doing my best to maintain, so I wasn't about to carry on like some jackass just because some dude I didn't know said the word *family*. Twice. Besides, Jesus didn't get this kind of reception at Christmas. So no, I didn't do any cheering that that day. I did, however, find my way to the *hors d'oeuvres*. Somebody went all out. I must've downed a whole tray of crab puffs by myself. They were the perfect munchies cure.

Nobody expected the hoopla to last forever, but no one saw it getting anywhere near as bad, near as fast, either. By Friday, just four days after the family speech, we were demoted to lepers, orphans and ginger-headed step cousins, twice-removed. Jeremy and I held off on the usual rooftop rituals until after. Good thing, too. They hadn't called the caterer on this one, though it might've made some of what they told us easier to swallow. The big brass showed up once again, but it was truly amazing how much the world had changed over the last four nights. Monday they couldn't say enough about how fucking wonderful everybody was. Friday we all sucked. Our readership had never dipped this low. Ever, apparently. And subscriptions weren't the only thing in the toilet. The bottom line was afloat with turds, too. Monday could've been a fairy tale for all the good it did us four days later. By day's end, more than half of us were handed our walking papers—six hundred forty-two of us, to be exact—including me, Jeremy, and even a couple of those Pulitzer Prize winners. Even they weren't good enough to survive a cut like this one.

That's what I heard, anyway.

Folks like me and Jeremy wouldn't know *them* if they tackled us in the hallway, yanked our pants down, and spanked our asses over piles of yesterday's news. Such was the pecking order. Working graveyards on copy desk will do that. So long as no corpses stood up and demanded a retraction, our work was cake. Otherwise, we were ghosts. Invisible. They had pretty-boy reporters and columnists to spare, but not one of *them* knew we even existed.

That didn't stop us from piling into Paddy's Pub with the rest of the varsity squad later that night, however. In our expulsion, we finally got to sit with cool kids. Not *with* them, exactly. Nearby was a better description. Still, it was closer than I'd managed in any of the previous fifteen years I'd worked there. All the tables were taken by the time I arrived, and of course, Jeremy messaged me right about then saying he'd be late. After waiting a half hour to get a beer, I thought seriously about leaving. The cool kids weren't nearly as fun as I'd imagined.

Then I spotted Jeremy. He practically ran to me, waving these papers over his head.

"I've got it! What we're doing next."

"What?"

"This! We were meant for this."

His waved his papers mere inches from my nose. Between his bouncing and the scarcity of light, I couldn't see a thing. I snatched his pages and walked over to a Pabst Blue Ribbon sign. The picture was horrible—worst I'd seen since the mid-1990s, when digital images first emerged—but unless I was seeing things, it looked an awful lot like the Alamo.

Public auction, it read. Submit bids now! Darville ISD, Darville, Texas.

"Where the fuck is Darville?"

"It's where I grew up," Jeremy said. "Well, not grew up, exactly. Spent a couple summers with a great aunt as a kid. I might have a cousin or two still there. But that's not important. What is important is that it's a nice place. It'll be a nice change from the city."

"Who said I want to leave the city?"

"I don't know about you but I sure as hell can't afford to live here without a damn job."

He had a point. The *Post* gave us a so-called "buyout," roughly half a year's pay. Fucking joke is what it was, and not a good one. It wouldn't last long. Especially not if I opted for another beer. Paddy's was mighty proud of its beverages.

But move clear across the country to some little shithole in Texas? I sure wasn't sold. Not after living on the East Coast for as long as I had. Still, Jeremy wasn't easily deterred. He tried a new tact, speaking with enough hope to cheer up an entire children's cancer ward.

"It'll give us a chance to do what we always wanted."

"*Oh?* What's that?"

"Have our own writing studio, a place to work with other writers. It'd be our very own Paladar."

There he went with that nonsense again. Ever since Jeremy and I went to that writer's conference a few years back, and that's all he'd talked about. Paladar this, and Paladar that. It got downright irritating after a while. It was in Iceland. The lodge was set on this mile-high crag overlooking a lighthouse and the better part of the North Atlantic. With these misty purple mountains at our backs, we ate fresh lobster every night as we gazed down at the raging sea below us. Couldn't have found a better place on the planet for word geeks like us. And work paid for everything—well, *almost* everything.

Work covered Palador's fees—any conference on the East Coast, they said—and surprisingly, Palador was way cheaper than any place in the states. By almost half, in fact. Our boss drew the line at flights, however, and those costs were astronomical. But Jeremy took care of that, too. We hitched on with a fishing crew, which wound up one of the best parts of the trip, almost better than Palador itself. We spent five days at sea total, there and back. They even wound up paying us, just for pitching in.

"I don't know," I said.

"What's not to know?"

"We're not the type of people who just *buy* buildings. You might recall, we're not exactly men of means, nor are we what anyone might call 'gainfully employed.' Where are you going to get the money?"

"I've read about people who landed old buildings like this for as little as a dollar," he said. "But the money's not important. You're missing the point. Just *look* at the place. It has all kinds of character."

"It looks like the Alamo," I said. Somebody had to.

"*So?*"

"If you remember your history, shit didn't go so well for them boys."

"They weren't us," he said.

I told you he wasn't easily deterred.

"How'd you find it?"

"You don't think I actually scanned newswires eight hours a day, do you?"

I didn't know what to say to that.

"Even if we got it, what makes you think anyone would come? That's where Paladar made all its money. And sorry, but I doubt many people in Darville spend much time looking out at the North Atlantic as they guzzle wine and host lobster shell wars."

"C'mon, man. I thought you'd be thrilled. Why you gotta shit all over it?"

I was pissing him off. That wasn't my intent.

"Look, man, we don't need to chart our futures tonight. We're supposed to be drowning our sorrows at the loss of this chickenshit job. How about I grab us a couple of beers, maybe some shots, and we write this day off the books?"

Like someone flicked a switch, he was done.

"You're on," he said, smiling his toothy grin.

"What's that saying they got about the Alamo?"

"Remember the Alamo," he said.

"Well, tonight we're gonna drink until we forget that damn thing," I said.

That toothy smile again.

"Forget the Alamo," he said. "I like it. So much so, I got the next round."

Although I contemplated leaving not long after I arrived that night at Paddy's, we shut the place down once the drinks got flowing. I'm not exactly positive, but I think we wound up at a table with one of those Pulitzer winners before the night ended. I can't say with any degree of certainty, of course, but that's how I intended to tell the story later.

I didn't see much of Jeremy after that night, though. Didn't give him much thought, honestly. I had shit to do. Besides, after seeing his ugly mug every day for the last decade and a half, I was rather enjoying the reprieve.

If he was still miffed about me not diving on the bandwagon to Darville, I couldn't tell. He was a hard cat to read sometimes. I wasn't out of line, I don't think, asking my questions. Even if I was, I wasn't losing any sleep over it. Besides, *Texas?* Neither of us would ever be mistaken for an oilman or a cowboy. Now was the time to be practical. Get back in the saddle, those Texas boys would probably say.

The first days after that infamous Friday, I slung a dozen or so resumes to various newspaper contacts, but it was pretty much the same everywhere. Nobody was hiring. Most were letting people go, with nowhere near as generous a buyout program as we got. After hearing how a couple buddies fared elsewhere, I learned to keep that part to myself.

By week's end, I was bored out of my skull.

Even in a city that size, there was not a lot to do for someone who lives life at night. TV sucks, I don't care what premium cable packages you might have. I leafed through a couple books I'd been meaning to get to, but nothing about them held my interest. No wonder they collected dust for so long. I even contemplated hitting a museum, or maybe going to the zoo. I read in the local entertainment guide about this impressive Bob Hope exhibit, including miles of filing cabinets filled with every joke he and his writers ever wrote, even the bad ones no one ever heard. He kept everything, apparently. Of course, it was closed when I was awake. No point in rearranging my routine just to take in a few sights, Hope or no hope.

Besides, my routine was already fucked up.

I'd been a daily reader of the *Post* for decades now. Hell, I learned to read in its pages. But the first thing I did after I got home from Paddy's was call up the paper and cancel my subscription. I swore I'd never look at another story they wrote again. Not after they booted me. They'd be sorry they got rid of me. I'd launch a boycott, make sure no one ever bought that shitty rag, ever again . . .

By the time I sobered up the next day, I'd talked myself out of all of it. I was even sorry I'd killed my subscription so soon, and because I'm pretty sure I called some old lady a whore cunt hose bitch for aligning with those fuckers from the fourth floor, I was leery about calling back to get it reinstated for the rest of the month. Be my luck, she was the only one still left to man the phone line.

It was a lot like quitting smoking. You've got every good reason *not* to, but you still spend the better part of your idle moments thinking about it. It was an addiction of the worst sort. No matter how I despised them, I couldn't help getting an eyeful of their headlines anytime I walked past a newsstand. And they were everywhere, here in the city.

So, I was glad when the lease on my pricey downtown apartment ended in a month. I certainly didn't have many more rent payments left in me. I'd called my dad in North Carolina and pretty much resigned myself to moving in with him until I figured out what to do next. I'd even heard about this online graduate school program that seemed worth checking out.

I'd bide my time in school for a couple years, and once those newspapers bounced back, I'd be welcomed back with open arms and pay raise for the degree. Little did I know, such days would never return. Those institutions of truth and justice I'd known all my life were done. Dinosaurs becoming fossils. We just didn't know it yet.

Between packing my shit and getting the car ready for the ride, I'd stay busy enough. I hoped I would, anyway. Turned out, I was right for once. Truth is, I could've used an extra week, when it came time to go. Amazing how much junk we collect whenever we get comfortable someplace. I already stowed most of it in a rented U-Haul when the phone rang. After a month without so much as a kiss my ass, it was Jeremy. He spoke just nine words and hung up.

"I got it!" I'll call when I get settled."

I still thought Jeremy was nuts, and not just goofy, funny nuts. No. I'm talking full-blown, he has a prescription, nuts. News has a tendency to attract folks like us. I knew, too, that Jeremy would keep his promise to call, even if it was some more weird cryptic shit, like his last call. But I was also certain that whatever he said to me then, whenever it was he called, those would be the exact words I needed to hear at that given moment.

He had a knack for shit like that.

✛ ✛ ✛

Of course, he'll probably start hammering at me to get my shit packed and get my ass on over to Texas. And you know what? I'll probably go, too. *Why?* Because unless my world makes some drastic turns toward fame and independent wealth over the next few weeks, what the hell else have I got going on? At least there, flop or fail, someone wants *me* in on the ground floor of something for a change. Even if it was some pipedream, in a wreck of a place we're going to wish a bunch of Mexicans would shoot us for, it'll be ours, to make what we make of it.

Even if it does look like the Alamo.

And who knew? Maybe I can learn a thing or two about how to dream. Worth a shot, right? And if all else fails—if nothing else remains—ol' Jeremy always did have the best weed.

My Little Girl

my little girl
turned 21
today

not *my* little girl
actually
delicate intricate

step—as it
were but still
my little girl

taught to read to write to draw
cook and sew, ride a bike, build a fire, too
my little girl

until the divorce

then it was me, I suppose
credited for affections
bruised purple and blue

tears *anger* hatreds despised
sometimes I'm glad I can't see
my little girl's eyes

still, my little girl
turned 21
today

and I can't even
call her—
my little girl

Gonna Eat This?

I've never had much use for a little dog. Not my thing. Most of mine are a hundred pounds or better. I've always preferred breeds that at least *looked* like they might have my back in a bar fight. Hico, my current beast, is no exception. She looks impressive, anyway, but she's a lot more likely to drown somebody in slobber, licking them to death, than inflict any real harm. Once she gets to know you, that is. Until then, you're on your own, I suppose.

Good luck!

Hico's part German Shepherd, part Boxer, and part whatever hopped the fence the day she was conceived. I'm convinced Daddy had to be the leaper because I met her Momma the day I picked out Hico. Momma didn't even get up when I, an absolute stranger, walked up and started man-handling her pups. A lazy, pampered critter, if ever there was one. I'm glad Hico turned out nothing like her.

Most of her siblings looked like wolf cubs, the shepherd strong in their features. Not her. Between that bulbous head and chopped nose, she was the most obviously Boxer of the bunch, nearly all white except for the blotches of cream on her back and the top of her head. Looked like she came with her own saddle and beanie cap, I remember thinking. And while she might've been just half the size of her siblings, she didn't take shit from nobody, even if she did spend the better part of her time tripping over paws that looked about four sizes too large. I couldn't help but smile, just looking at her.

Hico might've fit in the palm of my hand the day I brought her home, but she grew into those feet. And then some. Five years later, she's got a chest broad as mine, solid muscle, and she's tall enough to look me dead in the eye, if she takes walking about on her hind legs. Plus, she can launch herself a good six feet in the air. Just for fun. Makes most folks leery of the four-foot fence that surrounds my yard. It's why I'm pretty certain her Daddy had to be a leaper. That, or she's part kangaroo. She's about as smart as a sack of hammers—never has figured out she can clear that fence without trying hard—still, nobody ever sticks around long enough to test the theory. Not on *her* block.

It is *her* block, after all. She may not get much in the way of mail, but she'll let you know if you're not welcome. Along with me and anybody else within about half a mile. In fact, she'll give you six kinds of hell until you're gone. Truth is, I don't like people much, anyway, and so long as she stays where she belongs, I'm happy to let her motivate folks past my place in any manner she sees fit.

Beats her standing by, tail wagging, when a burglar finally does pay me a visit. That's for sure. In fact, she's good at keeping all sorts—salesmen, repo men, Jehovah's Witnesses—at a good damn distance. So she isn't a complete imbecile, I suppose.

Call me spoiled, but I've had dogs that could all but pour me a beer. Had one as a boy, a massive German shepherd named Major, that could lay down a full-grown Brahma bull by latching onto his nose whenever that bull got a bit too froggy. Had another in college, a Siberian Husky we called Me-Boy, that kept pace with me on a bicycle, never leaving my side even when I set land speed records down the backside of some mammoth San Marcos hill. He'd even stop at crosswalks, wait for the light to change, and check both ways first before walking out into traffic. Lot more than I could say for half the numb nuts I went to school with. More than once, he yanked one of them dumbasses out of harm's way, and never got so much as a pat on the head in thanks. Helluva lot more than I would've done. Step off in front of an oncoming truck like some kinda moron, and you deserve to become a hood ornament.

Of course, Me-Boy always was a better man than me. He'd wait for me, hours on end some days, while I attended class, and if it was a good day, he'd even lure in some unsuspecting doe-eyed sophomore. You know the type: "Oh, what a cute dog! You must be lost. Aren't you a pretty boy? Wanna come home with me?" All the while, he's sitting there thinking: *Nope. I can tell already. You're coming home with us . . .*

Good dog!

Of course, I don't have much use for a dog that plays chick magnet anymore. Not at my age. I don't need one tagging around with me wherever I go, nor one that can wrangle some ornery old bull. Still, just because a dog *barks* doesn't exactly make it gifted and talented.

Hico will bark at damn near anything. Somebody's walking by. There goes the garbage truck. A *cat!* There's the garbage truck, again. Once more. And again. Or my favorite: "Hey . . . Hey, man . . . It's *hot* out here . . . You gonna point that hose at them flowers all day, or you gonna cool *me* off?"

If you learn to listen, you can pick out what each of those barks means. "Hey, shoot the hose at me" is this embarrassing, high-pitched *yip* that sounds like a poodle farted through a kazoo. Crying shame such a noise could even come from a dog her size, especially when your biker buddies pull up. You plumb wanna crawl under the pavement from the embarrassment.

I can't help but smile, though.

There's the choppy, *the-puppies-are-missing bark*, usually in concert with some other hound (or hounds), clear across town. You can almost make out each dot and dash of their canine Morse code. Then there's the throatier, stouter "*BA-*

ruff!" she slings at most passersby. It's the *this-is-my-yard-so-you-best-keep-walking* bark. Works like a charm, most days, especially when you toss in that tremendous leap of hers. Few and far between are those who loiter on *her* block. Finally, you've got the *break-out-straight-jackets, aliens-have-landed, ninjas-are-on-the-roof* bark. It's about five parts wolf pack, three parts Rottweiler and two parts *get-your-ass-out-here-and-help-me-you-bastard!* She barely breathes. It sounds more like a dog fight than dog bark.

Dog *fight* was what she went with this one night, not so long ago. Which prompted me to wonder: *What the hell's her problem?*

It wasn't her first night of said racket. No sir. She'd already pulled this crap three nights in row. It being night four, I was about ready to pull an ol' Yeller and get me a *new* damn dog. Go ahead, call me what you please. But after stumbling my half-asleep ass out back, pitch dark, half-dressed and plenty pissed, never finding a damn thing but a minefield of fresh turds (barefoot, no less), and her, falling silent the second I set foot outside, only to start barking her fool head off again when I finally managed to doze off again, I was impressed she'd made it this long.

So, I wasn't about to do that crap again.

Plus, on this night, it was early still. Not yet ten. If somebody truly was messing with my dog, I'd love to catch them. Neighbors might think she casts a pretty mean shadow, snarling like she does, but trust me: She ain't shit. Remember what I said about on-coming trucks and hood ornaments? You stupid enough to mess with my dog, you're gonna wish you had it that easy. She might be a brainless beast, but she's *my* brainless beast, by God.

Rather than attack the problem head-on, like before, I opted for a new tact. I snuck out front, all but invisible in the darkness with my long-sleeve navy work shirt, dark jeans, and black ballcap pulled down low. Aside from a couple trees in the front and side yards, the house itself was the only obstruction to my line of sight. Poke your head around the corner and you can see a hundred yards in any direction. I keep it that way, for occasions just like this.

But upon doing everything I just described, I don't see shit. Not a thing. Nothing.

I grab a beer from the cooler on my front porch, and ease around the house to the carport. And it's there, beside the truck, I finally see something: This big band of light sweeps across the yard, disappears, then pops back up several feet away.

Son of a bitch, I thought. Aliens really *have* landed!

I'm standing there, watching all these lights flash on and off, listening to all these *bangs* and *clatters* and *grunts* in the back of my yard, trying to decide what to do next when my dog breaks off in an all-new level of unhinged. This time, however, rather just lights, I see what looks like some dude swinging a big stick over the fence at my dog.

Oh, *hell* naw!

I'm halfway across the yard, thinking up every one-liner I've ever heard so I can crack off something really cool before I whup this idiot's ass, when all at once, the shadowy figure with the big stick bolts off in the opposite direction.

That's what I thought, you son of a—

Before I can finish that thought, my dog's taken up residence in the opposite corner, way off on the other side, raisin' an all-new round of hell. *What* the . . . ?

Even over Dog Fight over there, I still heard it: *Thud-thud-thud* . . . Shadow Man, with the stick, who just took off the other direction moments ago, comes clumping back out of nowhere, clear on other side of my neighbor's place, right where the dog's snarling like somebody's nightmare. Took some rather fancy footwork to dodge the lights when they swept the yard again, so I hook for side yard, make my way up the fence line.

Then I hear it again: *Bang, Clatter, Rustle-Rustle, Grunt.*

I still can't make out what, exactly, is going on—it's just too dark—but I stay at my approach, ever closer, just as silent as a catfish passes through a shadow on the riverbank. Not more than eight feet from the action, I figure my eyes are still trying to adjust. Maybe they just didn't believe what they were seeing. Because it sure looked like Shadow Man yonder was taking up one of those mastodon-killing poses you always see in the picture books about cavemen. He cradles that big ass stick of his, aims and lunges in this ridiculous pirouette. Then he resets, spear ready. Aim, carefully, and *lunge!* Spin like an idiot. Rinse and repeat. Toss in Hico sounding more like a pack of jackals than a single animal, it sure wasn't helping me sort out the very strange reality I'd somehow stepped into, just crossing my yard.

I'm within arm's reach of Shadow Man before I can finally make out enough of his profile to tell that idiot prancing around his yard in the dark, stabbing the hell of his tree with what looks to be every inch of that proverbial ten-foot pole you hear about, is in fact the man who owns said house. My neighbor, still fully engaged in whatever the hell he's doing, is trying—unsuccessfully, I might add—to pinch one of those long metal flashlights between his ear and his shoulder, spotlighting some random branch in the tree, all so he can hop back in his mastodon stance and try that whole stab-twirl thing once more. Takes another one of his careful aiming sessions—you'd swear he's now trying to sneak up on said tree he's poked and prodded a dozen times—before I realize what that "spear" of his actually is: He must've sat there, ten minutes at least, screwing together wooden paint poles—the kind you use with one of them rollers to paint the ceiling or a wall, maybe—just so he could run around his yard, acting like a complete lunatic.

Now before I go any further, you gotta know one rather important fact: My neighbor—him and his wife, both—are *cops.* That's right. Badge wearing, gun-toting, law-abiding police officers. Can't count the number of times I've seen them strutting around like peacocks at morning's first light, about nine guns apiece strapped to various body parts, climbing into their cars to go to work. So here's a dude who has more guns in his house than I have hair left on my head—and surely enough pull to get away with discharging any one of said firearms within the city limits, if it ever came to the nut-cutting—prancing around his yard at ten o'clock at night, jabbing this long ass stick into a tree. And not just some simple *poke-poke-jab*, like somebody who punches a timeclock. No. He's all-out focused—I'm talking full-on trigonometry, advanced calculus *and* quantum physics focused—up at this tree, taking up his mastodon pose once again.

What started as a rather urgent situation has completely devolved into one of the weirdest nights *ever*. Just fuckin' *strange*. I back up a step, so he has plenty room with that stick, and then follow his light up into the tree. With Hico, still losing it, I try to spot what they both seem to think is up there. I search, hard, for several minutes, kinda worried at this point that one of the dudes I know will drive by, and, later, ask me what kind of jackass parade I was hosting the other night.

Thing is, I don't see a *thing* up there. Nothing. Not one goddam thing.

I've had about enough of this shit. Course, I'm still close enough I could lean over and give the ol' boy a kiss, if I wanted. I ask him, not real loud but loud enough, I guess:

What the fuck are you doing, dude?

Now I'd made no effort to sneak up on him. Not at this point. In fact, I'd been there long enough I figured he'd at least *smell* me. I may have stepped into the twilight zone here, but I'm pretty sure I also stepped into a few of those landmines my dog left for me earlier. Add in the hundred-degree heat, the pack-and-a-half of cigarettes I'd smoked that day, and the open beer I still had in my hand as I stood there peering up at the poor defenseless tree, I can't imagine not having some sort of odor about me at that point.

If I did, *he* never caught it.

Ol' boy come up off the ground about a foot-and-a-half, all while executing this perfect chess piece move. I ain't talking something simple, like a pawn or bishop or some crap. No. This was intricate. Complex. Like one those Ls the knights make, about two yards left and three back, all made mid-air with a perfect right angle in the middle. Or maybe like that switcharoo deal you do with your king and rook. That pole of his was the only thing still standing where he'd been just seconds ago. And sure, having a two hundred-pound biker with a beard past his nipples suddenly appear out of nowhere could be understandably unnerving.

But this dude's a *cop*. Surely, they get training for shit like that.

I'm guessing he skipped that day. You'd have thought I really *had* bent over and kissed him, straight on the lips. All I saw was whites in his eyes. "Pa-pa-pa—*possom*," he stammered, pointing up at the dark sky.

Protect and serve, my *ass*.

Still, I tried to act like he hadn't just screamed and wet himself like an infant. I looked back up at the tree, starting at the trunk and following each branch outward, one by one, while ol' Mastodon Mike fetched his flashlight and possum killin' pole once more.

I finally spotted him. The possum, that is. *Big* bastard. He looked somewhat relieved I'd disarmed the stickman, but a whole hellova lot of pissed off I'd let it go on this long. Mike found him with the flashlight at about the same time. He thrust his stick once again, missing entirely, but trying hard not to twirl like a fairy this time. He pulled back, jabbed once more, and missed again. Reminded me of this boy I saw once down near the border, who'd snuck out his momma's best broom to get at the piñata his pops had hung in a tree. No matter how hard he tried, though, damn thing was always just out of reach. That's what my neighbor looked like with that stick. Sucking his lip, flustered. It was kinda funny but *sad*, too.

Took him long enough, but he finally hit pay dirt, catching that big rat bastard in the tenders right below his ribs. Knocked him into a freefall directly above our heads. I stepped back, but Mr. Oblivious is busy yanking his big stick now, having lodged it somehow up there. Got it stuck pretty good, from the looks of it. Thankfully, the possum latched onto the last possible branch. Our intrepid warrior never even noticed.

My dog is plumb insane at this point. She's either telling all the other dogs within earshot to get over here quick to check out this dumbass with the stick, or she's seriously pissed this ugly, stinking varmint would dare climb in *her* tree.

Hard to tell sometimes with a dog like her, I don't care how hard you listen . . .

Mind you, this ain't my first rodeo with a possum. I hold them in about the same regard as snakes. Some folks, I hear, keep snakes as pets, in the same house they live in themselves. They gotta word for people like that: Abso-fuckin'-lutely crazy. That's what it is. A good snake, in my opinion, is one that's turned into hatband. Or a belt. A wallet, perhaps.

Just like snakes, they eat eggs, fresh out of the chicken. Chickens, too, probably. If you let them. So, they gotta go, plain and simple. They're ugly as sin. Looks like an armadillo fucked a swamp rat, and thus, life was born. Plus, they got an attitude to go with them awful looks. They're mean as hell, especially when they're hurt or cornered.

He's fully recovered from his recent freefall, that stick to the gut must've pissed him off because he sounds this wicked hiss and charges down the branch, straight at my neighbor's head. He acts like he isn't even aware there's an angry critter headed for his face. He's still farting around with that stick.

Thing is, I don't think it's an act. He really *doesn't* know he's about to get skull-fucked by big-assed possum.

It's headed right for him. Four feet. Three feet. A foot-and-a-half.

One of us had to do something.

I guess I could've fallen to my knees, prayed that the Good Lord smite this hideous creature before he injured a good and decent (but clueless) man. Or, I suppose I could've asked that his suffering end swiftly once that possum got hold of him, ask that God guide this noble beast's jagged claws with a well-placed stroke across the man's jugular.

Instead, I grabbed the branch, buckled my knees, right as he was almost on my neighbor's head. The limb bent. A lot. Even the possum's eyes go wide, right before I let it go.

Three things happened when that limb snapped back up: 1.) That cop finally got his stick free of whatever orifice he'd gotten it stuck in; 2.) My dog instantly stopped barking like her ass was on fire; and 3.) Perhaps most important, that possum launched about twenty feet in the air in a steep but oddly slow-motion arch. It was a thing of beauty, I tell you. And I swear, that critter looked like he was trying recall those plans he'd seen once on how to craft your own grappling hook. Or was it a parachute? Either would've been mighty handy right about then.

He landed in the middle of the street, hitting the pavement like a wet sack of bricks. Despite an obvious stupor, he wasn't stupid: He tried like hell to run. All he really did was stumble-step his way in a circle right back to where he started. Having paced his trajectory, I was right there when he hit. Ready. Sank my boot into his flank, sending him sailing into the hurricane fence across the street. I popped my lock-blade from my back pocket as I zeroed in once more, sinking it into his tough hide two or three (or twelve) times in rapid succession, right there in the street.

After all the evening's barks and grunts and glancing tree

stabs, it was suddenly eerily silent. My dog had wandered off across the yard, possum no longer in *her* tree, all humped up in her shitting stance like we weren't even there.

I'm pretty sure my neighbor, the cop, might've shit himself a little, too. He stood there, mouth hanging open, looking horrified. I guess he figured we were gonna *talk* this possum down from the tree. Meet him later for drinks so we could maintain our relationship. Maybe even part ways with a therapeutic and healthy hug.

He obviously didn't grow up on a farm.

I felt his eyes on me, so I took my time, wiping the blood and viscera from my blade into those nasty work jeans I had on. I even held the blade up to the nearest light, peering, intense—first one side, then the other, as if grading a fine wine—before clicking it closed and sliding it back in my pocket. I reached down then, never rushing, nonchalant, and I grabbed the possum's tail. It was still warm, leaking his life juices in a black pool at my boots. I hoisted him up, looked the sorry carcass up and down, then turned back to my neighbor.

I couldn't resist. I held it about head high and asked, "You gonna eat this?"

He stared back, horrified, as though I'd just murdered his first-born, clutching that absurd stick of his like his life depended on it. His mouth wide open but completely incapable of making a sound just then.

I shrugged as I turned back to my house, smiling in the darkness, flipped that carcass over my shoulder, and walked back home. I made it half a block by the time I stepped onto my driveway and finally looked back. The cop hadn't moved an inch. Hadn't closed his mouth yet, either. I tossed the dead animal in the trash bin, glad tomorrow was trash day, and walked inside. I have no idea how long he stood there, mouth agape. He never made a peep, but when I went back out for a smoke, about hour later, his house was silent. Dark.

I've lived here nine years now, and never once had a conversation with that man. Despite there being just a four-foot fence between us. Not once have I ever heard a snide comment about how tall my grass has grown or how loud those Harley pipes can be at two in the morning or how I oughta keep the Metallica to a more reasonable volume when I get home that time of day. Not one word—from him or anybody else in my neighborhood—and I couldn't be happier. Hico doesn't seem to mind a bit, either. Hell, if I'd a known it worked so well, I probably would've kept me a possum as a pet, a long time ago.

Trained him to eat snakes. Make wallets out of their hides. Or something.

TROUBLE IN PARADISE

Paul knew Janice was pissed as soon as he rounded the corner. She crossed her flabby arms in that same deliberate, exaggerated way women had used since caveman days, probably. It was a particularly handy means of insinuating their feminine dissent to most things manly across vast distances, effectively broadcasting their disapproval across many miles without her having to leave their young and walk all that way just so she could call him a dumbass to his face. Of course, most of them still made the walk anyway because they had to hear with own ears what their menfolk could've possibly been thinking. Paul watched her shift weight from one leg to the other, realizing at once that the new hip placement allowed her to strike a far more imposing glaring stance.

She had that body language thing down pat, Paul thought. It's no wonder she'd been junior high principal as long she had. On the plus side—if there *was* such a side after he just slapped down several thousand of his hard-earned dollars to get out of the place they'd dragged him seven hours earlier—but if there was a plus, Paul figured it had to be that the years didn't rob Janice of *any* of her dramatic flair.

She obviously had more than plenty still on reserve. He'd have to remember to tell her that later.

Partly because he was more than ready to get the hell out of there—he was just about sick of putting up with these jackasses already—but mostly, because it dawned on him, watching Janice carry on like she was on the other side of that reinforced plate glass between them, that dramatics had absolutely nothing to do with her demeanor. She really was about ready to blow a vein, which meant she was going to be a real pain in the ass until she calmed the hell down. And that wasn't going to happen for a while, Paul knew.

He could tell by her hair.

She'd always worn it short, but she kept it especially short during her years as principal, a look she somehow made even tighter to her scalp by means of a tight bun. Made her look like a real hard-ass, most days. That, or an Eastern German dominatrix. Either way, none of the kids in their hick town had the slightest notion what to do with either, especially not in seventh and eighth grades. She served as principal at that school for forty-three years, long enough for her to deal with the grandchildren from her first class of students.

When she finally passed the baton on to someone else almost a decade ago, she took that bun out. Not now, though. No, Janice had that damn thing in so tight she couldn't blink.

Paul had grown accustomed to it after so long. He must've missed it earlier. He probably wouldn't have noticed it now were it not for her fierce face in the glass, glaring at him like a hawk ready to swoop down on field mouse.

Paul tried not to look directly at her. He couldn't handle her being that serious. Not just then, anyway.

But she never eased up, not even when some skinny fellow showed up—a bondsman, probably—handed her what appeared to be a full ream of copied documents from their transaction. That skinny fella beside her was talking to her and pointing at things inside the packet, but Janice refused to break visuals with Paul. The man tossed up his hands and finally walked off. Janice, her enraged eyes still on Paul, tucked that packet to her hip so it wouldn't come apart on her and there she held it, like a schoolbook.

It reminded Paul of the *Encyclopedia Britannica* volumes he kept in handy reach of his easy chair, back when Janice and the rest of the bunch were just kids. Anytime he heard one of their spats get going, he'd grab his book, open it to whatever page, and act totally lost in the article when they got there. It nearly always followed this exact pattern: There'd be some loud *THUMP!* resonating through their hardwood floors, followed by some muffled voices and some half-hearted tussle behind closed doors. Then—one, two, three, *CREAK!*—that door flew open on a four-count you could set a watch to, somebody'd squall *I'm gonna go tell!* and off they went, stomping down the entire hallway.

Something about the sight of Paul, poring over that big, thick book, always kept the kids at bay. Often, it turned them around, right there, or, they'd go find Mom, bypassing him altogether. Kept him out of the fray, anyhow. Annie, getting dragged back by whoever came to fetch her, gave him some fowl looks, but like the kids, she never bothered his reading, either. Funny thing was, he couldn't even guess how many times those pages wound up in his lap upside down. Fixing the problem would've found him out for sure, so he sat there, staring at upside down pages for however long it took.

"Alrighty, bub, let's stop right there," the jailer said, yanking on Paul's cuffed hands like he was at the world tug of war finals.

His arthritis screamed as the kid cop jangled his keys behind the old man for what seemed like half a day before he finally stabbed the lock and freed the cuffs. Paul rubbed his wrists. They'd been on since breakfast.

"Open sixty-four," the jailer said into one of those shoulder-mounted police radios, which seemed about as necessary in *that* jail as hourly conjugal visits with a one-legged Thai hooker in full riot gear. The place currently held three inmates, one of whom—Paul—was about to be freed. Of the remaining two, the youngest prisoner was a sixty-eight-year-old jail trustee who had full run of the place, whenever he wanted. Of course, he was sound asleep right then. The other, eighty-four, couldn't sit upright for more than about ten minutes before he had to lie back down. Paul couldn't imagine what the hell he must've done to land in here. Only thing he could figure was it happened some time back.

While the officer strutted about like a peacock, waiting for the door to open, Paul couldn't help noticing how tubby, soft and pimply this kid was. Hell, at ninety-four, he could take this guy, and he'd probably have to take it easy on him when he did. Sad what they considered viable lawmen nowadays. Paul looked over at a pale woman with a jaw full of gum, staring back at him from inside her door-controlling cubicle, sizing him up with each open-mouthed smack. She took her sweet time getting to the lone button on the console in front of her, but finally pressing it and after several seconds of buzzers, the actual door finally popped open.

"Stay outta trouble," the kid said. "I don't want to see you back here again."

He stood there, holding the door open and staring off to nowhere. Took everything Paul had to not deck the shit out of him. He glanced back at the woman in the box before he walked out. She was busy staring at her nails, still smacking that gum. In a place that held just two prisoners, most days—six, tops if all hell broke loose—Paul couldn't help wondering who the hell she had to fuck to land the job as door opener in that place.

That woman was a fixture in that office, though, that much was obvious. She sure wasn't heading off anytime soon, that was for sure. Damn shame she got any money to not do a damn thing all day. Unless, of course, they paid her per annoying smack. If so, she was at risk of hitting overtime territory already. What got him even more, there wasn't a single tool in her work area. Not a single piece of other equipment even accessible. No phone, no fax, no computer—nothing at all—and sad part was, she wasn't all too attentive at getting said door open. That was tax dollars at work for you though, Paul was certain, and he couldn't be happier they were all getting pay raises again this year.

That door wasn't even all the way open yet when Janice lit into him.

"What the *hell*, Daddy?"

Paul didn't acknowledge her, just shuffled his geriatric feet, still rubbing his wrists.

"Of all the things I *never* expected, bailing my ninety-four-year-old father out of jail was—"

He wasn't listening. Not then and not there. They had the whole ride back for that.

He pushed open the police station's front door and stepped out into hot afternoon brightness. Squinting, he spotted Jerry's minivan, its engine whining to keep the A/C pumping. In an otherwise empty lot, Jerry had taken the lone handicapped parking place. Other than him being a bit of a retard all his life, he had no ailments to warrant him parking there. Paul shook his head as he climbed in. His heart just wasn't into setting Jerry straight. Not that day. In fact, he didn't say a word for the rest of the ride.

Everything was hunky-dory until the entire clan arrived, uninvited, in the middle of last month. They came, supposedly, to celebrate his ninety-fourth. That's what they all told him, anyway. Thing was, not one of them brought him a single gift or a card. They brought bag after bag of grocery items from their cars. Nothing Paul could use, of course. The kids ripped apart the chips like they'd brought in empty bags. Everything looked like they'd all hit the same gas station on the way out of town. The real kicker, judging from everyone's noncommittal answers, was no one realized they'd missed his birthday by ten days. In fact, his birthday fell on a whole other calendar page. He sat around last weekend wondering if anyone would remember. They didn't. He didn't even rate a phone call or even a Hallmark moment. And now, here they were. Cutting into his fishing time.

What's more, he hadn't heard from any of them since they laid poor Annie to rest. Nine months ago. Yet here they all came, not so much as a phone call. Just as he was checking the line to his favorite fishing rod, the first carload pulled up. Paul didn't recognize who it was until they climbed out. They'd bought a new car since he'd seen them last. They stretched and carried on like they'd been in that van for hours. Unless Jerry and Janice bought a new house someplace out of state to go with their new van, he knew the ride from their place to his was no more than twenty minutes, tops. Damn thing must be uncomfortable as hell, he thought.

Just one fact was certain: Paul would've rather gone fishing.

Don't take that wrong. Paul loved his family. Absolutely. He devoted the bulk of his ninety-four years to them, in fact, something he wished they remembered a bit more. No one called since the funeral, nor did anyone lend a hand in the previous eight years, when Annie wasted away with the cancer. Thanksgiving came and went. Then Christmas. Easter. When he didn't hear a peep from anyone on Father's Day, he wrote them all off.

Why they chose *that* day, he couldn't fathom.

They barely got in the door before her boys flopped on the furniture, each one staring at a goddam cellphone and whining about how bored they were. The rest disappeared in the back and started rifling through dresser drawers like it was rummage sale. His youngest boy Joey—who finally pulled up in his Mercedes five hours behind schedule—even had the nerve to hit Paul up for gas money, so him and that fruitcake little *friend* of his, *Javier*, could make it back home. You'd think a couple retired college professors would have enough brains between them to budget some travel money, but what could you expect from two grown men who still pretended they went home to separate houses every night?

"I'll just add it to that graduate school bill you always swore you'd pay back someday," Paul said, sliding his son a couple twenties. Would've thought he doused them with a bucket of warm piss, the looks they gave him.

By the time they got around to cutting the cake and flashing their pictures, thirty-seven people had piled into Paul's house. The sun had already set, and his head throbbed from all the noise. It took him a full week to put everything back in its place. When the last set of taillights pulled out his gate, it was the best thing he'd seen all day, even if it had cost him forty bucks, that fancy silverware set he'd gotten as a wedding gift and never used, and the bulk of his late wife's jewelry.

But it was worth it. They were gone.

If he'd had the good sense God gave a mule, he would've packed up and moved, right then.

Paul should've realized something was up when Janice pulled up to his house, alone, two weeks later. A thunderstorm blew through earlier and cooled it off nice, so he took advantage of his porch swing. She climbed his steps, all smiles. He waved at her, but never got up.

"How are *you* doing, Daddy?" she asked, far louder than necessary. She patted his hand, then flopped her sizable ass beside him. Totally killed that comfortable sway Paul had going.

"Surprised to see you back so soon. Come for the Tupperware?"

She snickered. "Oh Daddy, stop it . . ."

Janice kept up the small talk for several more minutes

as they swung back and forth, enjoying the scenery. Butterflies flitted around the flowerbeds sweet Annie planted years before. Chickens scratched at the back fence. His small Angus herd grazed off in the distance. The storm's last remnants still darkened the horizon. The more they sat there, the more Paul's suspicions melted away. It was nice, sitting and chatting with his little girl on the front porch. They used to do it all the time, back when she still had pigtails. Seemed like every day, she'd have these grand adventures to tell him about—something happened to a friend at school or in a book she was reading—it didn't matter. She'd tell him all about it. It was their own special time together, all those years ago. Before he knew it, the old man threw his arm around his little girl, even if she wasn't near as little as she used to be.

"Daddy, there's something we need to talk about," she began, her tone suddenly dead serious. "Me and the family have been talking since we were here for your birthday—"

"Family? You mean that pack of hooligans you gathered up here a couple weeks ago? You do realize y'all *missed* my damn birthday, *right?*"

Janice didn't acknowledge him, and she surely wasn't smiling any more. Not in the least. She went from daddy's-little-girl to junior-high-school principal in the blink of an eye. Forty-three years in a profession like that will do it to most anyone, Paul figured. Still, one thing was certain: She hadn't come here to fill him in on the goings-on in her life, relive old times, or talk about all those fish he'd yanked out of the pond. She had a mission.

"What would happen if you tripped and fell out here someplace? No one would even know you're hurt."

"Maybe if you came to visit more than once every nine months—"

"It's not good for you to be out here all by yourself all the time. You need to be around people. Get involved in things. Spend some time with your friends—"

"All my friends died a long time ago."

"Make some new ones," she said, standing up to face him. "You're losing every social grace you ever had since Momma died. I mean, that *awful* thing you said to poor Joey the other day—you know, he's still upset by that?"

"What? That he ought to pay back the money *he* says he owes me? Sonofabitch! Him and that little *boyfriend* of his been showing up here in friggin' *luxury* cars for years now—"

"See? That's exactly what I'm talking about. You're just flying off the handle and cussing like sailor for no reason at all. *Healthy* people don't act that way. And when's the last time you went to the doctor?"

Paul had been ready to fire back, but that last question stole all his wind. He hated doctors. Always had. Besides, he'd had it up to here with those bastards over the last few years, dealing with Annie's illness. Seemed like they were forever going here to see *this* specialist or there to make *that* appointment. And look at all the good it did *her*. She spent the last eight years of her life wasting away to nothing, barely able to get out of bed.

Janice turned and walked toward her car. "I set an appointment for you with my physician next week. I'll be by to pick you up first thing Tuesday. You better be to ready to go when I get here."

The old man spat over the railing as she pulled away, still sitting in his porch swing. His little girl never once looked back.

Paul couldn't sleep worth a damn the night before his appointment. He went to bed early and even set his alarm for the first time in decades. All he did was toss and turn. Shortly after midnight, he got up to get a drink and pee. Instead of wandering back to bed, he plucked a book off the shelf and tried reading a while. The book was one of those so-called *gifts* Joey insisted he read several years back: something called

Anti-Intellectualism in American Life, probably written by some Yankee Jew. He suffered through the first few pages but wound up tossing it aside. That book made his head hurt. So damn dull it was like watching grass grow. Thing was, Paul actually *liked* watching his pastures get taller.

He walked to the kitchen, set some coffee to brew and sat at the table to wait. He checked his watch, smiling as he thought back to an old TV ad he'd heard years ago, "It's 3 a.m. Do *you* know where your children are?"

Same thing must apply to old-ass parents, too. Why couldn't they just let him alone?

That doctor's appointment turned out to be a hellova lot more than he bargained on. They must've drawn about three quarts of blood, and poked and prodded every orifice he had, at least twice. They even put him on a treadmill with all these doohickeys and wires taped to his skin. Paul would've loved to have seen his fat ass daughter plod along on that thing, wearing one of those damn hospital gowns for all the world to see. After they finally let him get dressed, they put him in a room and had him work puzzles for the rest of the afternoon while some goon sat there with a stopwatch, jotting notes on a yellow pad.

The Army wasn't even this thorough, and he'd earned Silver Stars for killing Nazis and Japs with them.

By the time he was done, it was almost five o'clock. He was exhausted and starving. They hadn't let him eat anything all day long. Paul never uttered a single complaint, though. All he cared about was getting back home.

Despite his day-long battery of tests, the old man noticed something else, too. Two things, actually. One, Janice couldn't stay put more than five minutes for all the phone calls she was fielding that day, always waddling off someplace else for privacy. Two, he hadn't seen an actual doctor all day. Nurses and techs everywhere, but not one doctor. It wasn't until the place was about to close that some kid in a tie and long white coat walked up.

"Mr. Jamison, I believe?" he said with an annoying nasal twang. "Hello. I'm Doctor McCloud. I'd like to go over your results, if you don't mind."

If it got him any closer to getting back home, why the hell not, Paul figured. The boy rocked on his heels, arm outstretched like he was a porter in front of some big city hotel. Paul shrugged and trudged down the hallway in the direction of the man's arm. What's a few more minutes after a day like the one he'd already had?

The office was the very last possible doorway they came to at the end of the corridor. Even Janice was puffing by the time they took their seats in his posh leather chairs. The doctor sat behind this mammoth hardwood desk, barely more than shoulders and a gleaming shaved head. He had one those annoying little Fu Manchus, perfectly sculpted on his lip. He looked even younger, tinier, behind all that furniture. He perched his yuppie half-frame reading glasses on the end of his nose and began flipping pages in the file Paul had accumulated through the day.

"Hmm," the doctor said, his scrawny finger sliding down the report. By the look of him, he'd never done an honest day's work in his whole life. "I *see* . . . Interesting . . ."

The old man glanced over at his daughter. She sat there, purse in her lap, watching the doctor just as cool as a clam. Either she'd been through all this before herself, or she knew something Paul didn't.

"So, what's the verdict, Doc?" Paul asked.

The boy doctor leaned back, tossed his tiny spectacles onto the desk. "Well, I got to tell you, Mr. Jamison. You're a surprisingly healthy individual for a man of your age. All your blood work came back good. Your heart and lungs are in excellent shape. Even your prostate exam checked out good.

If you don't mind my asking, exactly how old *are* you anyway, Mr. Jamison?"

Paul didn't say so out loud, but that question actually *did* bother him, quite a bit. The first thing everyone he'd seen that day, right after getting his name and temperature, was how old he was. He'd been fielding the same question all day, with each new nurse that walked in the room. Buy a *real* pair of glasses and you might've seen that, he thought.

"I'm ninety-four." Paul said.

"My God! I know people who are *literally* half your age who could only dream of being as healthy as you are . . ."

"Sounds good. Thanks a lot, Doc." Paul was already scooting his chair out to leave when the boy behind the desk spoke again.

"But I'd be remiss if I didn't tell you about what we found with the brain scans and memory tests you did this afternoon," he said. "According to our tests and our interviews with members of your family, I do believe you're exhibiting some early signs of Alzheimer's disease—dementia, some people call it—to be honest, it has me, and several members of your family, I might add, concerned about your continued wellbeing—"

If Paul had been about fifty years younger, he'd have leapt across that big ass desk and strangled the crap out of that pompous little boy-man peering back at him from behind all that wood. "*Early* stages?" the old man sputtered. "I'm ninety-fuckin-four-years-old! How many more years you think I got? Sure, my memory ain't what it used to be, but you just said yourself—I'm healthy as a horse—so I didn't play your little card games as fast as you wanted. Who gives a holy Goddamn shit?"

"I'm afraid I'm going to have to insist you refrain from such language," the doctor said. "In fact, I think it might be wise for us to consider something more in the form of permanent care arrangements."

As if she was waiting for her cue, Janice started rummaging through her purse. She pulled out all these colorful brochures, fanning them out on the desktop like a professional blackjack dealer. The pages were filled with all these smiling silver-haired codgers, waving at one another as they strolled the expansive grounds, dining at what looked like some snooty-falooty restaurant, or happy as hell to be building a goddam birdhouse in some arts and crafts class.

Paradise Manor, it read. Senior living at its finest!

"You're just going to *love* it there, Daddy," his daughter told him.

What truly pissed off Paul was that while he'd been wasting his day at the doctor's office, the rest of his darling children were packing him up for the move. Hence all the goddam phone calls, as best he could figure. They even dipped into his bank account, he would later learn, so they could prepay for a full year in advance. Plus, after he hiked the half-mile to get to this damn doctor's office, a nurse appeared not long after that brochure session with a wheelchair. They weren't letting him out of there on his own accord. He never even got to take a shit in his own toilet or go to sleep in his own bed, just one last time.

They took him straight to Paradise without so much as bite to eat.

And wouldn't you know it? Their kitchen had closed by the time he arrived. He choked down some stale vending machine crackers that must have been packaged during the war. Suffice it to say, the years had not been kind.

Paradise Manor looked positively nothing like the place in the brochures.

It might've once, but Paul doubted it. More likely, the place in the brochures had to be in another state someplace, if it truly existed at all. The grounds were not kept in the least. Everything looked shabby. Paul had nicer looking cattle pastures and barns back home. And there certainly were no smiling senior citizens out strolling about, like the ones in the photographs, waving to everyone they met. The only folks he saw when he came in were a sad forgotten lot, slumped over in their wheelchairs, facing bare walls, and smelling like they hadn't bathed in about a week. That posh dining hall didn't exist either. Instead of linen table cloths and elaborate place settings, like the ones shown in the brochures, all the cafeteria held was a few wadded napkins, some left behind Sporks, and a wad of green Jello someone either lobbed onto the floor or dropped on the way to the trash can.

He was so hungry he half-considered scooping up that glob of Jello from the floor as they pushed him past. Meanwhile, Janice yammered her fool head off at the tired charge nurse who was obviously not thrilled about his late arrival.

Pale blue walls with little more than a hospital bed and a side table with an ugly brown plastic chair shoved in the corner was all Paul found of the advertised "posh accommodations for every lifestyle" from the brochures. That's when Paul noticed his personal possessions, scattered here and there, too. There was the picture of Annie he'd always kept beside his bed, his razor and toothbrush set on the bathroom counter, a jar of red, white and blue lozenges that Annie had put there the year Reagan became President. Some asshole even brought that crappy-ass book he'd tossed aside the night before.

"Well, we're going leave you to it, Daddy," Janice said, backing out of the door. "You sleep good now, and we'll be by to visit you real soon."

Paul was downright ravenous by the time breakfast rolled around the next day. He couldn't sleep worth a crap on that plastic mattress they'd given him. Back home, he normally got out of bed until about eight. Here, he was already showered and shaved by six. He headed over to the cafeteria as soon as sun kissed his windows, trying to make the most of a bad situation. He 'd always worried his kids might gang up on him like this, but Annie insisted they establish that trust for the farm, just in case. They'd named Janice executor, her the eldest and most responsible of the lot.

Fine lot of good that proved to be.

Paul's first disappointment of the day came in the fact that they don't serve coffee in Paradise. Apparently, that stuff was poison to some of their patients.

"That caffeine will land you in an early grave," some wire-thin, stressed out 30-year-old had the gall to tell him as she helped the more infirmed patients with their plates.

A few of these fuckers would probably welcome such a fate, Paul thought to himself. He knew *he* would, anyway. It would probably be his first day in the past ninety years that Paul would start his day without that morning cup of coffee. He even managed a daily dose on the front lines of the war.

Disappointment number two, they served no seconds. Hungry as he was, he probably could've downed fourths that morning, but all they gave him was an ice cream scoop of imitation scrambled eggs, two slices of turkey bacon, and a stale English muffin.

"There's a strict policy on portion sizes around here," some other passing orderly told him, pointing to a pile of brown bananas and two withered oranges over in the corner. "There's a bowl of fruit over there if you're still hungry."

But the real capper of the day came when Harry Truman wheeled his chair into the room. Not *that* Harry Truman, of course. *That* fellow'd been dead for almost fifty years now. Paul only *wished* that *this* Harry Truman had died a long time ago.

"Looky what the cat dragged in," Truman said. "I guess they let just any ol' piece a trash in this place nowadays."

"Morning Harry."

"I see ain't nobody told you the rules in this here place yet. That's alright. You always been kinda slow, anyway. I forgive you, *this* time . . ."

Just the sound of that man's voice made Paul's blood boil. He tried his best to focus on that orange he was peeling and ignore the bile spilling out of the old man's trap. But it wasn't easy. Truman kept his voice low, so only Paul could hear what he was saying. Everyone else in the room seemed oblivious.

". . . You's sitting at my table, see? So, what you need to do is move move yo' ass on over to someplace else. Go grab you a seat over there with them niggers—that's where a sorry piece of shit like you belongs anyway, nigger-lover . . ."

Paul gathered up his things. He'd scarfed his plate in no time flat, anyway. He could eat his orange wherever, and anyplace seemed a hellova lot better than here, dealing with *this* asshole. Paul slid his chair back and slowly rose to his feet. Before he stood all the way up, though, the withered old man in the wheelchair reached out and grabbed his arm.

". . . Hey *boy*, since you up already, why don't go fetch me my plate? That's a good nigga job for you. I'm gonna make you my bitch. Be just like old times for you . . ."

It happened so fast, no one saw it coming, not even Paul.

His fists were already clenched before Truman latched onto him, and that last round of comments certainly didn't calm him any. Paul wasn't sure if it was Truman's sudden and bony grip, the words he was saying, or just his cesspool of a life in general. No sooner than Truman got the words "old times" out of his mouth, Paul felt himself spinning around fast and planting a solid right hook across the old man's jaw. Truman's dentures skittered across the floor. A fount of blood erupted from his nose. Other patients stared with open mouths full of half-chewed eggs, petrified.

"Call the police!" a portly nurse hollered back to the cook. Two large orderlies who looked like bouncers at a biker bar appeared from nowhere and shoved Paul to floor as Truman grabbed his nose.

"You fucked up now, boy. I'm gonna own your ass . . ."

Paul tried to keep his eyes focused out the side window for the duration of his ride from the jail. If there was anything worthwhile about his time behind bars, it was that he managed to talk the deputies out of a cup of coffee. It couldn't have tasted any more like toilet water, but it was better than nothing.

His daughter was still blabbering away in the backseat. She hadn't stopped bitching since she climbed into the backseat of the van. The old man still hadn't said a word.

As he watched the passing trees and fence lines, he saw a little country church approaching. Funny how life will sometimes press all your buttons at once, Paul thought. Out behind that old church, beneath this monstrous tombstone, lay the love of his life. It wasn't Annie, though she'd been a good wife to him. She was buried clean on the other side of the county. And no, Paul never cheated on his bride. Sweet Annie was his first and he'd stayed faithful to her until the day she died. All seventy-six years of their marriage.

Here lay the remains of his sweet Georgette. Although he never so much as kissed the girl, he just knew they were going to spend their lives together. But it never came to pass. A fence line was all that separated her family's farm from his, but it may as well have been the Grand Canyon for all the good it did him. Though they may have played side by side as toddlers, even sharing the same washtub on more than one occasion, a pall wound up falling between them, not long after Paul and Georgette began school.

Her daddy died rather unexpected one day following a brief bout with what everybody took for a cold back then. To keep the family fed and the farm going back then, one of Georgette's uncles came to stay at their farm and fill her late father's shoes. Rumor had it, he helped himself to lot more than the dead man's footwear and place at the table, but people didn't speak of such things back then. Not at Paul's house, anyway. But he was hardly welcome around their place either, not like Georgette's daddy had been, that was for sure. The man drank a whole lot more than her daddy ever did, a fact that surely must've taken more than a few crumbs from the family table on account they all took on a rather ragged appearance in the years that followed his arrival. Georgette and her siblings seemed to live in fear of the man. A no-account if ever there was, Paul's daddy would say whenever the man came around, spitting as he said it as if to get the taste of the words from his mouth.

Yet it wasn't the man's drunkenness nor the fact he was letting their farm go to ruin nor that he did whatever it was he did to Georgette's mother and the kids to make them all fear him so that was whispered in the swirl of local gossip. Rather, it was something that man said one day in town during one of his drunken outbursts about Paul that seemed to stick in everyone's minds like ants trapped in cedar sap. It had to do with Paul's complexion and, no doubt, his naturally curly hair. Even in the well-tanned state of everyone's arms back then, a fact that everyone came by naturally from all the field work that had to be done, Paul's was somehow darker than the rest. And despite both his parents looking as white and Irish as folks could possibly get, the boy's unnaturally dark skin was a sure sign he had some slave in his lineage, somewhere down the line.

That's what Georgette's uncle surmised one day in some drunken ramble, anyway. And damn the luck if those words didn't stick like Gospel. Just like that, Paul couldn't have gotten any blacker if he changed his name to Sambo. And heaven forbid, especially back then, any respectable white girl be caught dallying with some colored kid from down the road, no matter how poor a family she might come from or how lovely a young lady she might grow into one day.

Paul shook his head and looked away as the memories washed over him. His eyes lighted on the arrest report his daughter had tossed into his lap, not long after she climbed into the van and launched into her bitching session. It was then he realized how much that particular report looked like another he'd been handed, so many years before.

He couldn't keep that smirk from curling his lips.

"What the *hell*, Daddy? Are you *smiling?* I guess getting tossed in jail for beating up a little old man in a wheelchair is somehow funny to you . . ."

Truman hadn't always been so little or old. In fact, he'd been quite the bear back in his younger days. A real jock, captain of the school football team. Although he and Paul were the exact same age, Truman towered over Paul for most of his life. The only thing larger than the man's brawn had been his big-ass mouth.

Truman had been an asshole all his life. A bully when he was a kid, and a spoiled fucking brat when he got older. Still, everyone around these parts knew and respected the Truman name. Not only did he claim to have some distant relations to the fellow with the same name in the White House back when, but you couldn't hardly toss a rock in their hometown without hitting something his father owned. There was Truman Hardware. Truman Grocery. Truman Feed & Farm Supply. Truman Land and Cattle Company. Rumor had it, his daddy even owned part of the bank, the barber shop and the funeral parlor. No matter if you were coming are going, his old man had figured a way to make money off it.

Truman didn't get a lick of his daddy's business acumen, nor had he picked up a single bit of the elder man's good nature. He didn't have to. His father's fortune saw to that. About the only thing he was good at was lording his wealth over every other person who crossed his path. Paul had grown up a scrawny little kid, one of six sons of a poor dirt farmer. His family couldn't even afford to buy shoes for school. They barely had enough to eat, most days. The Great Depression moved in and stayed awhile over at the Jamison place. Not surprising, after the Japs bombed Pearl Harbor, Paul wasted little time joining the Army. He stuck around just long enough to help his family plant their cotton crop, but when he was done, he thumbed his way to San Antonio to enlist.

Not a moment passed, however, that sweet Georgette wasn't on his mind.

Paul watched her grow from a sweet little girl to a gorgeous young woman. He was smitten since they'd first met, and he was pretty sure she liked him, too. Although there was a steady line of suitors, especially when she got to high school, she kept everything casual with her dates. Being a shy boy, Paul never once dared approach her. Besides, all the shit her damn uncle had started about him. He'd wait until he had made his mark on the world, saved a bit of a nest egg, and sweep her off her feet one day. And the Army was the best chance he had of ever making that happen.

Boot camp was a breeze for Paul. He was no stranger to hard work, and he was already a crack shot from having relied on his rifle for food, growing up. He even ran into a couple fellas from back home, who kept him apprised of all the things taking place back at their little patch of South Texas. No surprise, Paul figured, ol' Truman had hopped on the military bandwagon with the rest of his classmates. His daddy's bankbook, of course, landed him in officer school. Everybody else from back home was just an enlisted schlub.

But none of that would matter now. With graduation day quickly approaching, Paul couldn't wait to get back home and make his proposal to sweet Georgette.

He should've known, even at that young age, life didn't always go as planned.

Sporting his freshly pressed uniform, Paul walked the streets of his hometown a new man. No longer was he that dirt poor, little farm boy he'd always been. And to hell with what people whispered about his lineage. He was a private, second class, in the U.S. Army. Little kids, tagging behind their mothers, would stop and salute him as he passed. He'd return the favor, the mother's lighting up with big smiles as he swaggered past. He wore his cap cocked to the side, like Humphrey Bogart in that movie he'd seen just before he started boot camp. He oozed confidence he never even he knew he had.

Although he signed on to kill Japs, the Army was sending him to Germany to shoot Nazis first. He shipped out to the frontlines in less than a week. But he needed to find Georgette. He'd stopped by the soda shop, where she used to work through high school, and even the beauty parlor. No one had seen her in days.

Still, if Paul was ever going to ask her to marry him, it was now or never.

He was on his way to the diner when he heard the engine slowing to the curb behind him. There, sitting behind the wheel of a brand-new Cadillac convertible, was Harry Truman, sporting his officer's get up, grinning like a possum eating shit.

"Ten, hut," Truman said, sneering.

Paul wanted to ignore him but knew full-well the man outranked him. After he'd been saluting the local townsfolk all morning long, he couldn't very well play like he hadn't seen the golden second lieutenant bars on Truman's chest. Not here in front of God and the world on the courthouse square, anyway. He grudgingly raised his hand to his head.

"That's more like it, boy. Officer on deck!"

Paul was so caught up in the public shaming he hadn't seen anyone else in the car. Not until now, anyway. There sat his sweet Georgette, a weak smile on her perfect lips. She gave a half-hearted wave, then returned her gaze to the dashboard. She looked tired, like she hadn't slept in days. Defeated, almost. Her makeup was caked on so thick, it took Paul a second take to notice her left eye looked a bit off, possibly bruised under all that Maybelline.

"Oh, I almost forgot," Truman said, as he stepped out of the car and walked up to Paul. "I'd like to introduce you to Missus Georgette Truman. We just got back from Vegas, tied the knot two days ago."

He flashed a big gold nugget ring on his left hand. Georgette turned away from the scene playing out in front of the car. She stared off in the distance like she couldn't believe it either.

Truman jabbed Paul in the ribs. "Well, aren't gonna congratulate me?"

Paul would've rather smeared fresh dogshit in Truman's face, but once again, he knew he couldn't show his disdain in public. Not to man who outranked him, anyway. He grasped the big man's hand and tried to manage a less-than-heartfelt "good for you."

Even those words caught in his throat.

Truman tightened his grip and pulled Paul close, nearly hugging. His normally thunderous voice was barely a whisper: "You didn't think I noticed you pining away for her all these years, did you? Looks like the better man won once again, don't it?"

Truman chortled like he'd just heard the funniest thing in the world, and to him, it may well have been. He finally released his grip, slapped Paul hard on his back, like they'd been chums since birth, and turned to walk away.

"See you overseas," he said, returning to both his ride and his bride, though the ride clearly held his genuine pride, of the two. "Try not to get yourself killed out there."

Paul spent the rest of his time back at the farm before he shipped out. It looked like his family might finally make a decent crop, provided those springtime hail storms stayed away. He never spoke a word to anyone about what had taken place in town when he got back, but everybody knew. Truman had stolen away every last shred of dignity Paul knew of home before he'd be asked to go kill for his country.

Leave it to Army to make sure everybody in Europe would know what happened as well.

After weeks spent digging foxholes, shooting at man-sized targets on the range, and learning how to kill a man with nothing but your pinky finger—all at which Paul had truly excelled—his commanding officer decided a potato peeler would be the best weapon in Paul's hands.

"Report to the officer's tent," he was told. "You drew KP."

And who'd he run into the next day at chowtime?

"Looky what the cat dragged in. I guess they let just any ol' piece a trash in the Army nowadays."

Originality never was one of Truman's strong suits, but he managed a few laughs from the tagalongs in his entourage. Most everyone else just grabbed their trays and sat down to eat, but Truman wasn't done yet. Despite being one of the junior-most officers gathered there under the mess tent, he decided to pull rank on Paul once again.

"Ten, hut!" he yelled, snapping to perfect salute himself.

Paul stood there, peelings hanging off his arms. Mind you, there were captains, majors, full bird colonels, even a brigadier general, already seated in the room. Not one of them had put on any airs when they grabbed their plates. They looked at Truman like he'd lost his goddam mind. Some colonel from the Bronx took pity on Paul.

"At ease, lieutenant," he said. "Hurry up and grab your grub. We got a lot to do today."

Truman did as he was told, but Paul felt the man's eyes burning right through him the whole time. He and his cronies took a table near the back, taking their sweet-assed time. Most of the officers who'd gotten there before him, including Colonel Bronx, were already clearing out. By the time Paul was wrapping up his shift, Truman and his merry band of assholes were the only ones left.

Paul was sweeping up at the service line when the big man pulled a photograph from his pocket and passed it around. "That's the sweet little piece of ass I got waiting on me back home," he said.

The rest of his crew jeered and whistled as the picture made its rounds. Truman stood up and started walking toward Paul. The rest of them got up, too, like they were tied together with string.

"Can you believe that little Nancy right there and me come from the same town?"

His voice was booming now, the closer he got.

"Yeah, he used follow that girl around like a lost little puppy all the time." His crew laughed, which worked like gasoline on Truman's fire. "I hear the little shit even had some fucked up notion he'd marry her someday." They laughed some more. "Turns out, though, he wound up just standing there with his tiny pecker in his hand. Her uncle didn't think twice when a real man came calling her . . ."

That's how it happened, Paul thought. All that no-account probably saw were dollar signs when that jackass came calling, promising who knows what.

". . . Yeah, we got hitched up in Vegas just before I shipped out," Truman continued. "From what I heard around town, this little chickenshit was running all over the place trying to get his puppy dog act started all over again when he finished basic. Little did he know, the big dog had already got hold of his little bitch . . ."

His crowd laughed even more this time. Paul was disgusted. He couldn't believe anyone would talk like that about his own wife. Especially not *his* sweet Georgette. Truman and his cronies were barely five feet from him now.

". . . Yeah, she kinda of whimpered a bit when I stuck it in her the first few times, but I put that bitch in her place. Taught her some manners, know what I mean? Hell, I even had her sucking me off all the way back from—"

It happened so fast, no one saw it coming, not even Paul.

In the blink of an eye, Truman was doubled over, spitting out his front teeth, his nose gushing blood. His giggling gaggle of yahoos stood there, mouths open, no one daring to move or make a sound.

Paul got a month in the brig for that little stunt. They even demoted him, toyed around with the idea of a dishonorable discharge. They wound up sending to the front, where he spent the rest of his days in Europe dodging German machine gun fire. They did shit like that that when an enlisted man assaulted an officer, especially back then.

When he didn't get killed fighting Nazis, he volunteered to join the boys over in the Pacific. He fought through many a close call, even got to kill his fair share of Japs. It added another year to his enlistment, but what did he have to lose? Despite almost getting booted those first few days, Paul left the service a full-rank staff sergeant. He even got the Silver Star for valor. Twice. One from each theater.

Still, the best part by Paul's estimation was that he never saw Truman again during the war. Some days the fighting got so bad he wasn't sure he'd make it. Others were so dull he thought he'd die of boredom. He made some of the best friends he'd ever know and watched as countless others drew their last breaths. Some days he was surrounded by such beauty he knew he'd never lay eyes on such magnificence again. Others were so awful they still woke him up in cold sweats some nights. But of all the things he could've possibly brought back home as mementos of the war, Paul kept just one item: The offense report the MPs made him sign the day he laid Truman flat on his ass.

Never would he have guessed he'd ever get an updated version, not a few weeks after turning ninety-four, anyway.

Paul caught a ride back home aboard a Navy battleship when the war finally ended. Those final days turned out to be some of the most vicious battles. It seemed like every man, woman, and child was grabbing a gun to stop the U.S. advance. A week of calm seas was just what the doctor ordered for a man who'd spent the better part of three years sleeping in a hole that he himself dug. There was one night back in Belgium, when he and a few boys laid claim to an abandoned convent, but other than that, Paul had kind of got used to the stars as his blanket.

He visited his parents a while, but ultimately decided to head to San Marcos, where he attended Southwest Texas State Teachers College. There, he met Annie, the woman who became his bride, got his degree in vocational education, moved back home to become a high school ag teacher. The rest, as they say, is pretty much history.

Despite his officership, Truman returned home the same lout he was before the war. He blew through sizable portions of his father's wealth, especially after his parents both died within a week of each other. He even sold or otherwise shut down several of his daddy's business interests—Paul wasn't in the know on such things—he did his best to avoid Truman, whenever possible. Besides, the school district frowned on its teachers keeping with the crowds Truman liked to gather at the dives where he hung out, so it wasn't nearly as difficult as one might think, even in a town as small as theirs.

Truman attempted a smear campaign when Paul first came back to take over his teaching duties at the local district, spreading all over town how he was nearly kicked of the military for assaulting an officer. He particularly liked the phrase "dishonorable discharge" and used it a lot. Of course, Truman conveniently left all the circumstances of his claims, particularly the part where that little farm boy he'd always picked on had laid him out cold. Thankfully, the school principal stepped up in Paul's defense, even sent letters home to parents touting his war accolades.

When Georgette died a few years later from booze and pills, no one was terribly surprised. Rumor had it, Truman had a good half dozen girls on the side throughout their marriage. She tried leaving him twice, Paul had heard, and wound up in the hospital both times. Most folks assumed her overdose hadn't been accidental, though no one would utter such a thing for fear Truman might target them next.

Georgette was only thirty-seven.

Janice hadn't shut up once, the whole ride back from the jail. "Now I'm gonna have to talk to the center's administrator. I just can't believe it! And I tell you what, *mister*: You better *hope* I can smooth things out with her . . ."

Paul wished his hearing was worse. He would've turned off his listening devices a long time ago. Still, he had to admire her fortitude. It wasn't hard picturing her making a really good school principal. Oh, the ass chewings she must have handed down to hundreds of delinquents through the years . . .

As Jerry turned into the circle drive at Paradise, Janice finally fell silent. Paul glanced back at her to see what had happened. Her jaw hung slack, the color drained from her face, and her eyes, big as platters, stared straight ahead. He turned to see what she saw.

There at entrance to Paradise, sporting a poofy neck brace and what looked like a maxi pad taped to his face, was Truman. He sat hunched in his wheelchair right in front of the door. The center's administrator stood beside him, the same crossed arms and hip jut Janice had sported, back at the jail.

Not again, Paul thought.

As Jerry pulled to a stop, a crowd began to gather at the door. Paul saw that same tired charge nurse who checked him in the night before, pulling out what looked like his suitcase. There were the same two burly bouncers who had slammed him to the floor earlier that morning. And, still sporting her disdain with both arms, was the same center administrator Janice had just mentioned.

His daughter flung open her door and dove outside, bewildered. Her mouth was still hanging open. Would've sworn she was watching her house burn down. Paul clicked his latch and slowly swung a foot down to the pavement.

Before Janice could say a word, the administrator held up her hand as if she were working a crosswalk.

"I don't want to hear it," the woman told Janice. "What happened here today was totally inappropriate . . ."

"But—"

"No, Janice. *You* listen! We've got enough to worry about here without having to concern ourselves with patients attacking one another. We just can't have it. We're not staffed to deal with that sort of thing."

She turned, pointing at Truman. "Just look how he left this poor man. You're lucky he didn't kill him, hitting a little old man in wheelchair like that." He sat looking like Golem behind all his bandages. "And don't even get me started on how bad he disrupted our routine, or how terrified some of those who saw what happened still are . . ."

"Yeah, but—"

"But *nothing!*" the administrator fired back. This woman was *good*, Paul thought.

"I know we've known each for quite a while now, but this sort of thing cannot be tolerated. I had a meeting with the board of directors this morning. That was no picnic, let me tell you. We've come to the decision, in the interests of other patients and staff, that we will be terminating our obligations with Mr. Jamison, there. Considering the upheaval his actions caused this morning, it was also decided that he will be fined, I don't remember how much, but it's precisely the amount left on his balance. I'm sure those funds could be applied to some of the less fortunate we have here in our care."

Janice's shoulders slumped, her head slowly bowed.

". . . We've packed up Mr. Jamison's belongings here, so that you can take him home. Right now. If you wish to challenge the board's decision, there is a review process that I can send you some information about, but between you and me, I wouldn't waste your time. It seems to me if Mr. Jamison there has it in him to execute an unwarranted attack of a poor helpless individual like Mr. Truman here, I do not feel that he has any need services we offer anyhow, which is how I phrased it in the report I filed with the board, personally, myself earlier this afternoon. That report, by the way, carries a lot of weight with all the rest of senior care facilities around these parts, so I wouldn't waste your time trying to get him placed anyplace else near here anytime soon. And on a final note, we have filed a restraining order with the judge following this morning's incident. Should we find Mr. Jamison anywhere on our premises at any time in the future, he will be arrested for trespassing and hauled to jail. Combined with the elder assault charges we intend to file, should that event ever transpire, he would likely face a lengthy prison sentence."

Switching targets, she added, "Is that what you want, Mr. Jamison? To die in jail?"

"No ma'am," he told her, trying to sound as sincere as possible.

"I do believe this concludes our arrangements then," she said.

The charge nurse stepped forward with the suitcase, dead

silent, handing it to Janice like a soldier handing a folded flag to a widow.

"Good day to you," the administrator said.

All the eyes of Paradise glowered at Paul as Truman raised his withered claw.

"See you in the funny papers, *boy!*" he said.

Janice turned to load the suitcase in the van. As she did, Truman extended forefinger and thumb, forming a fake pistol with his hand, silently mouthing "I got you," so no one else would see. Paul swung his leg back in the van and pulled his door shut without so much as a goodbye or kiss my ass. For the first time in all his ninety-four years, he could've kissed that old bastard in the wheelchair.

Acknowledgements

Although several pieces included here were decades in the making, all were written between May 2017 and November 2018 during the height of Bobby Horecka's studies in the graduate creative writing program at the University of Houston-Victoria. The bulk of what you read here was submitted as his final program thesis, written under the direction of UHV's Diana Lopez and Beverly Lowry, for which he was awarded his Master of Fine Arts degree in December 2018. Copies of that original manuscript are on permanent file at the university library. Before any of these works appeared in a single collection, however, several were picked up as individual, stand-alone works in various literary magazines and anthologies. The following is an accounting of those publications:

Lubbock 1974

Originally appeared October 2018 in *Amarillo Bay* (Vol. 20.2), an online literary magazine published since 1999 by English Department faculty at the University of South Carolina in Aiken, S.C. The author worked closely with the publication's fiction editor Richard Mosely, professor emeritus in English and creative writing at West Texas A&M University in El Paso. Notification came that story would also appear in the anthology *Runaway*, edited by Luanne Smith, Michael Gills, and Lee Zacharias and published by the literary nonprofit Madville Publishing founded by Kimberly Davis in Lake Dallas, Texas, (2020).

HAP/HAZ/ARD

Originally appeared May 2018 in *Rise: Havik Anthology 2018*, edited by Jennifer Snook et al, published by creative writing students and faculty at Las Positas College, Livermore, Calif.

The Legend of Chunk

Originally appeared August 2018 in *The Central Texas Writers Society 2018 Anthology* (ISBN 7981721561636) edited by founding member Nicole Metts, published by the regional literary group based in Copperas Cove, Texas. It also was selected by *Down in the Dirt* for two 2019 issues, "The Deep Woods" and "The Flickering Light," put out by Scars Publications, founded and edited by Chicago author and poet Janet Kuypers.

My Little Girl

Originally appeared May 2018 in *Alchemy 2018: Magazine of Literature and Art*, put out by creative writing students and faculty at Portland Community College, Portland, Ore.

Mr. Man Candy

Originally appeared in the May 2018 edition of *Bluestem Magazine*, which has been published continuously since 1966 by the Department of English at Eastern Illinois University in Charleston, Ill. The May 2018 edition was edited by Olga Abella et al, and published online only, featuring both the text of the story and an audio version, performed in its entirety by the story's author. An excerpt of the story also was selected by *Down in the Dirt* for two 2019 issues, "The Deep Woods" and "The Flickering Light," put out by Scars Publications, founded and edited by Chicago author and poet Janet Kuypers..

Forget the Alamo

This story first appeared in the February 2019 edition of *The Ocotillo Review* (Vol. 3, No. 1), a literary magazine published by the nonprofit Kallisto Gaia Press in Austin, founded by author, poet and songwriter Tony Burnett. The author worked closely with the publication's fiction editor Jan Rider Newman, writer of short stories, poetry and novels, and editor and publisher of the *Swamp Lily Review*.

About the Author

Bobby Horecka obtained his MFA in creative writing at the University of Houston-Victoria in 2018 and taught introductory English courses at nearby Victoria College. He has numerous publications, including works of short fiction, prose, and poetry, in literary magazines and anthologies like the University of South Carolina's *Amarillo Bay*, Eastern Illinois University's *Bluestem Magazine*, the Austin-based *Scribe*, a monthly member newsletter put out by the nonprofit Writers League of Texas, and *The Ocotillo Review*, published by Austin's literary nonprofit the Kallisto Gaia Press, to name a few. Prior to his MFA graduate studies, Horecka spent 25 years in print journalism and currently writes for four newspapers in Lavaca County, Texas.

Lightning Source UK Ltd.
Milton Keynes UK
UKHW010051060620
364507UK00003B/711